LOVE TO DEATH

EMILIA FITZ

CONTENTS

This book is dedicated to my husband, Love of My Life. I had only two people close to me; my dear step-mother for my first twenty years, and my husband, Zbigniew Fitz, for the next fifty years — the only friend I ever had.

He was kind, talented, and full of wisdom. We struggled, shared aspirations — we became a symbol of what deep friendship and collaboration of the minds can do for the quality of art. I was loved, and I am grateful for that.

PROLOGUE

This is a story of love at first sight, the story of Emilia and Zbigniew Fitz. It took place in the real world, full of challenges. Only strong love could endure all that we faced. I started my memoir with the stories of our parents – how they did not survive World War II. Their stories made a great impact on our personalities. We grew up with the fear of war and hate of violence. Art became a way to show our thanks for life and a way to develop our minds, breaking down the walls of our consciousness. Beyond a love story, it is a story of loyalty, sacrifice and the search for meaning through art.

We met at our first year of Fine Art Academy in 1963, in Cracow, Poland. Our love for art united us and grew into a deep friendship, love and a lifetime collaboration in perfect unison. Our goal was to create history.

We came to the USA from Poland, via Paris in 1974.

We decided not to have any children (because of art) and not to have a permanent gallery, but to find our own style first. Since 2001, we had departed from narrative style, discovering the role of strong emotions (shock) in art – like a hammer for our brain. Our art became emotional-psychological. But the price for our achievement was a long-time struggle with ups and downs, starting with hunger in Paris, eating bread from the garbage cans after the rats.

We wanted to be ourselves when it came to art, and this caused us not to fit anywhere, even when we felt ready to face the art world. Works of art, paintings, became commodities and consumer goods. The art was only as good as your sales. To sell better art, you need to do a democratization of taste. New norms were created, and artists did what was in fashion. The consequence was democratization of creativity. It meant everybody could do it. To sell better, faster, art had to be easy – so easy that even a monkey could do it. What happened to natural talent? Individuality? Without the intimacy of brush and mind, humanity in art is lost. Art is dead. Where's the satisfaction from taking the challenge to do something difficult?

But there will always be the need in us to express disinterestedly our inside, our humanity, our joy and sorrow, like a need to sing when we are happy or sad. Ignoring individuality, somebody's uniqueness is to condemn to perish.

Share your best with others. Your art does not need

to fit a mold. We all have something unique to offer. Talent needs to be noticed, respected and preserved. We achieved high quality art. It is daring! Our legacy needs to be saved.

There is hope in every pain. Our art is a gift to the world. Take it, because I am not selling. That is my story. I am hoping for someone to see the real dimension of our passing through this earth, leaving the trace of love.

Praises for Zbigniew and Emilia Fitz Art and Emilia Fitz's Memoir Book

07/10/16

Dear Emilia Fitz,

Thank you very much for having such an interest in our collection. We apologize for taking such a long time to respond to your endearing letter. Your assemblage of images of works along with your book chapter is quite remarkable and your story is truly inspiring. We also send our condolences for the passing of your husband who was a beautiful artist. At our space, we only display works of art that the Rubell Family has personally acquired; we have no relation to the gallery nor publishing business. Remorsefully, we are unable to assist you at this time but sincerely hope you find that support soon.

Best regards,

Laura Randall
Registrar
Rubell Family Collection
95 NW 29th St.
Miami, FL 33127

Attachments: We thank you for your beautiful images and are respectfully returning them in hopes you can send them to an appropriate contact.

Praises for Zbigniew Fitz Paintings and Emilia Fitz Paintings

JAN. 13/2016

Work of Emilia and Zbigniew Fitz

As Emilia explained to us her story and the life she had shared with her husband Zbigniew Fitz, it is apparent that they were totally and completely dedicated to their art. There is a zealous devotion to art-making and a deep commitment to their practice and that seems to have been rivaled only by their devotion to each other. Speaking with Emilia, and reviewing images of her and Zbigniew's work, it is obvious that their art reflects a shared life filled with passion, pain and a curiosity to explore and push the creative process. Much of Zbigniew's work is raw, angry and filled with human emotion. Often, it is familiar narratives twisted into bold strokes of color, distorted disembodied limbs, twisted faces and intense grief, especially in the series painted in response to 9-11. There is an authenticity and sincerity in their art-making and I hope that Emilia, having lost her soul-mate and her muse, can channel that grief into her practice.

Nicole Gallo, Curator for Agnes Gund
New York

Praises for Zbigniew Fitz Paintings

Gmail - Saatchi Online - a message from Charles Saatchi

GMail

Zbigniew Fitz <zfitz76@gmail.com>

Saatchi Online - a message from Charles Saatchi

1 message

Wed, Nov 14, 2007 at 1:14 PM

Charles <yourgallery@saatchigallery.com>
Reply-To: Charles <yourgallery@saatchigallery.com>
To: zfitz76@gmail.com

Hello,

Very happy to see your work on Saatchi Online.

I am thrilled that the standard is so high from such a variety of artists and hope it will be interesting to gallery owners, exhibition curators and collectors to see such diverse work.

All my best,

Charles Saatchi

Fitz

From: "Larry Rinder" <lrinder@cca.edu>
To: "Fitz" <fitzsart@peoplepc.com>
Sent: Friday, September 28, 2007 4:28 PM
Subject: Re: Inq.

Hi,
I checked out your images online. The work looks fascinating. Congratulations on a remarkable body of work! I doubt that I can be of any help, career-wise. I'm, no longer in the curatorial field. Three years ago I became an academic administrator.
Best of luck,
Larry

Fitz wrote:

Dear Mr. Rinder,

We are so happy to find you. We are couple of artists living in South Carolina. Some time ago we sent you our portfolio to Whitney Museum. Now we have a second chance to bother you. We are desperate to show our art to you because you are somebody respected and caring for art. For a long time we lived in a kind of self imposed isolation, but now we are ready to face the art world and we are looking for a friend to help and advice.

Please, let us know how to send you our portfolio - we have everything on CD, but written material is hard to read , so maybe we can just send it to you via post office?

Anxieous to hear from you,

Sincerely,
Emilia and Zbigniew Fitz   fitzsart@peoplepc.com

No virus found in this incoming message.
Checked by AVG Free Edition.
Version: 7.5.488 / Virus Database: 269.13.33/1034 - Release Date: 9/27/2007 5:00 PM

TIME... TIME... TIME...
TIME AND US...

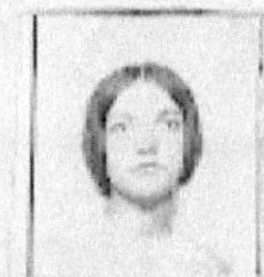
POLAND 1963

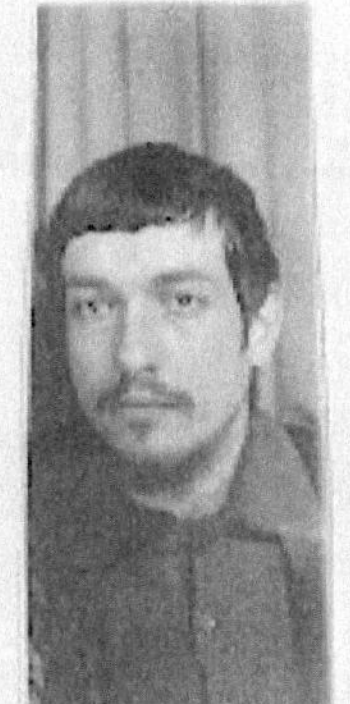
ZBIGNIEW PIT...
1968

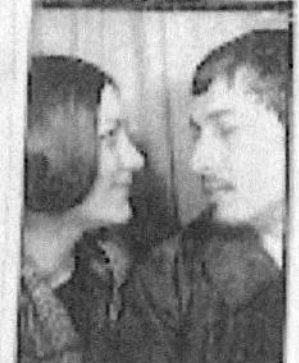

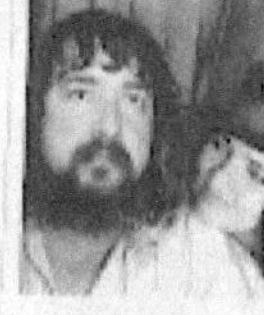

PARIS   1968

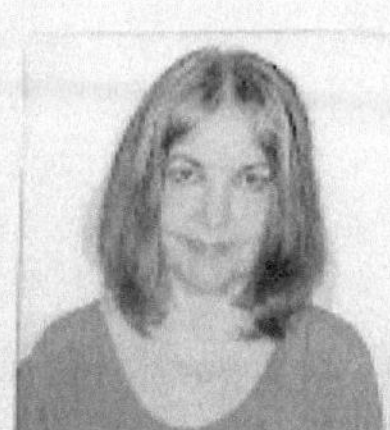

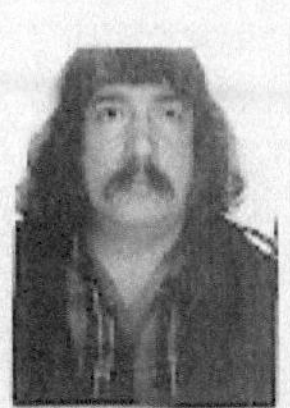

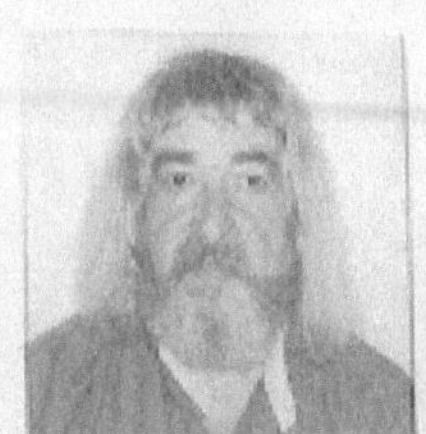

USA - 2010   USA - 1999   USA - 2013

ACKNOWLEDGMENTS

I would like to say thank you to those who encouraged me to write my story, especially to Connie Post, who gave me her precious time to type my characters. Also, I am grateful to Patsy Taylor for making endless amounts of copies. I am grateful to Laura W. from Newberry, SC, who patiently searched for answers to my questions online. I would like to thank those who read my book with teary eyes, assuring me that my story is deeply felt. I thank my old friends for encouragement to write, especially Helena H. from New York City, Eva W. from New Jersey, and Elisabeth H. from Phoenix, AZ. All these good people helped me to overcome my despair and turn it into something positive, to glorify my love story and maybe to give hope to others that true love is possible.

Big thanks for Al and Eve. Without them, I couldn't make a book. They are my best friends.

CHAPTER 1

BOTTOMLESS PIT

Joseph has been trapped. For the moment, he forgot where he was – he must have been asleep. He was numb with cold. His legs felt stiff, and he was in total darkness, like pitch black. The only thing he remembered was this fear…terrible fear. He was all a-tremble, fluttering. He felt the tightness of space around him. He had been dreadfully cramped. He made a comment in his mind, "there's no room to move much."

He decided to examine this surreal space, not sure yet if it was a nightmare. With his right hand, he touched his forehead covered in cold sweat. His breathing became faster. He fidgeted with his hands blindly, checking out the closest area. He stretched his arms to the right and to the left. It was a space about 4 feet wide. Quickly, he touched something cold, wet and hard like concrete. Another fraction of the seconds, and he knew it was enclosing him like a cage, but in a circle. Now, he knew…. he was in the well…

Coming back to reality, he asked himself, "Why is it wet? This well was dry and was covered for a long time." He stretched his hands again and realized it was just a little damp. "Just one spot. Probably I spilled some water while sleeping. But I'm cramped in this well, within narrow bonds. But I'm alive, am I?" He pinched himself to be sure about his reality.

"Yes, I'm alive. I am lucky."

He frowned, wanting to make sure his memory was still intact. "Yes, it's a war time. Germans killing people in masses. Especially Jewish. I am in Poland, in 1944. I came from Cracow, here to this beautiful countryside and became a countryman. My sweet wife brought me here to this village, to her family, to save me." He asked again, "why I am cold? I have a feather bed and several blankets. Oh, yeah. I am uncovered." He went deeper under all these coverings. He noticed, "this well is deep, so it is warmer here than outside. It's late spring time, but the nights are cold. It must be the night."

Suddenly, he heard voices. It was some distance, but he could hear they spoke German. He was frozen with terror. "Stop…. stay still…. don't move…. don't make any noise…. don't open yourself to a death blow." He repeated this over and over without moving his lips. Slowly, voices became more and more distant, farther away from the well until they faded and stopped.

"They left! Whew! Ohhhhh! Now my heart is palpitating. Calm down....sh......sh.... slow down.... slow down.... slow.... slow.... breathe." Now he was breathing with relief. He thought, "good people from the village were telling Germans that this well is contaminated with Typhus – it works. Since I'm here (several weeks), none of them approached.

He continued to reason with himself. "Why was I born Jewish? Well, you see, it could happen to anybody. But they don't know that, do they?" He smiled tenderly. "But I am lucky. I am married to this beautiful, Polish woman. Since Germans came to this small village, hiding me at the bottom of dry well was her idea. Her family is helping too.

Today must be a cloudy day or full moon – can't see the difference. The slits on the well's cover are too narrow. I better hide under the blankets." Here, he could use his small flashlight to take notes in a small notebook. He sighed. "Why did the Germans stop here? How long can I stay here? Okay, okay, stop your lamentation – Survive!" He murmured, "but it's so black, so pitch black."

Joseph had been trapped in this total darkness without a way out. Opening or closing his eyes didn't make any difference, but he closed them anyway. He lowered his head. "I want to penetrate this black. I want to face it." His only escape now was to descend into himself. He started to talk to himself without moving his lips.

"I am descending."

"It's noiseless…"

"I am going down…down…down."

"I don't see the bottom…"

"Is it like a well? But it's longer, narrower. It's a tube. It goes down. I follow."

"It's all dark, but I know the tube is here. So, I go. Down."

"Is it endless? Is it bottomless? Is it boundless? Is it termless?"

"I am afraid of the black and emptiness, but I have to know. So, I continue my descending. I refuse nothingness. I contradict this notion. I feel. Therefore, I am. I lost the notion of time. Time is not important any more. The essence is. I am."

"I don't know how far I went down, or how long it took until now, but I want to go to the bottom of my being. So, I continue….to go down… and then I had the impression that I am slowing down. Softly."

"Something is enveloping me, trespassing me. I am in a small space. I reached the bottom! I feel the presence, something is sleeping there…Peacefully… Lovingly…So, it is not endless. The tube of my being……. or is it? It's pulsating with security. It's a consolation."

"I have the notion that this silent presence feels like power. It's within me, but it's like a second, other me. Independent. It's something that knows better, works for me, can decide about my healing without me being aware. It's something that knows what I am and wants me to live forever. Something indestructible. If only I would not stay in a way, in any way, consciously or subconsciously."

"It is something I can trust."

"It feels good to BE."

"I feel safe here. I don't want to leave and go back to the outside world."

"What is that I feel? It is unattainable, subtle. How do I know it's real? I just know. There are certain things that you touch by your 3rd eye. Where is it?

"Listen to the silence. You will know. I feel there's more to that. Some poets or painters felt that. I don't want to go back to life outside of me But something drove me to open my eyes. I am looking up...Seeking..."

"I am stunned. I see a tiny dot, far up, like a light of hope. And hear a tiny whisper..."

"Joseph? Joseph."

He saw the light of a flashlight pointing at his face. "Sh," he whispered back. He grinned with joy. That was his wife. He never knew when she could visit him. She quickly pulled down the cotton cord with a pail full of non-perishable food and water. The best was dry polish sausage if she could get it. When he emptied the weekly supply, she pulled up as quickly as she could and disappeared. Between the slices of bread, surprise! It was a photograph of their one-year old son. She also gave a note.

"*My Love,*

Nobody can imagine how I miss you. The tears stick in my throat when I think how hard it must be for you to be in this dark all alone. But each time, when I glance at your son, the certainty comes upon me that everything will be ok. There are rumors that Russians will come and they'll bring freedom to us. I heard that Americans will help too. Somehow, they manage to start to send the boxes of food, whoever is lucky to get it.

Your son grows healthy. But don't worry, I used peroxide water on his hair. With his big, almost black eyes and curly gold hair, he is so cute that Germans are stopping often on the streets, all smiling and pinching his cheeks. At first, I froze with horror, motionless, with fear that they would recognize His Jewish face. But no. Joseph, my love, you need to be strong, for us. We need you. Everything will be ok. I can feel it. Kisses from your loving wife."

Joseph was staring at the photo of his son, in silence, and for a long time every day (dark day), with tears in his eyes. He knew he was loved. This gave him all the strength he needed. We never know how much we can take it, surpassing ourselves with suffering, we grow into the beauty of the human race. There's more in us than we ever could imagine.

I, Emilia, the author of this book, heard the story of Joseph only generally. But I imagined what one could feel being in such a situation, so inhuman, that my imagination couldn't follow it all. I tried to put myself in his place.

His child survived and grew up beautifully. This miracle child one day crossed my path like a prince from a girl's dream. He became the love of my life.

Joseph Fitz remained hidden from Germans for several months. He survived and left the well. One year after the end of The Second World War, he died from a heart attack.

CHAPTER 2

ALL TO DUST

My future stepmom, Ann, was born in 1915, (two years before the Revolution of Russia in 1917), near the small town of Gradimir in the idyllic countryside of Russian, which today is Ukraine. Her parents were peasants, making their modest but secure living on a 49-acre farm. In the post-Revolutionary, Communist Russia, they were considered as Kulaks, the rich parasites of society – their future was uncertain. They had five children, and they all participated in everyday life from early ages. They were happy, noisy, with pink cheeks, being in constant excitement about all little things. Ann, the oldest of five siblings, had no idea about living in paradise – she took all for granted without assuming if it all would stay forever.

"Bolsheviks are coming, we have to run, hurry, hurry! AAAAAANN...RUUUUUN!" That dramatic whisper awoke her. Mother disappeared in the dark of night. She jumped through the window without seeing anything – all she knew was that Gradimir, the small town, was North. She tried to whisper, "Mom, Mom," but nobody responded. It was like all family dispersed. In a panic, she ran through the fields faster and faster, until she was slipping, overturned and fell into the ditch. She lost her consciousness.

Early in the morning, Ann awoke shivering and cold. She was in the wet ditch. She came to herself quickly and whispered: "Mom…Dad…" She jumped out of the ditch and looked to the south, where her house was. In the horizon she noticed smoke going straight up. She shuddered with horror and started to run toward the house. Her heartbeat was rapid.

"Is our house burning? Did they burn our house? NO! It cannot be…No…No…Noko!" She kept running, the smoke wasn't too big, and it looked like it got smaller and smaller. But the closer she got, the stronger the smell was.

"What is it, this strange smell?" Finally, she was almost there and stopped and froze. The feeling of terror came upon her. No more farm. All burned away. All leveled to the ground. All immersed in black. From the ashes, debris stuck out. Black pieces of wood became smoldering ruins. She looked around and saw the trees had become stumps without a trace of leaves or bark, stretched naked in their black nonexistence. From the limbs, tiny chicken bodies were hanging down ossified in black form with beaks wide open in their last scream. Motionless.

Ann felt numb, frozen in a twilight zone where time had stopped. Slowly she turned her head toward the barn, also leveled to the ground, and slowly shambled forward. The smell became stronger and suddenly she understood what it was. It was the smell of burned flesh of all the animals unable to escape. Their black, stiffened bodies twisted in convulsions, with the scream set on the standstill of death. Cows, horses, pigs died in impossible pain to comprehend.

In a moment, she noticed the big body of the mama pig, now reduced to a dry mass of black. She looked like she tried to cover her piglets to save them, but they were so small. There was no trace of them left. She turned her head to the right side of the barn where she saw the ossified baby cow and the dog trying to save the baby cow, pulling her by her leg toward the door, but he also became stiffened, perished. That's what dogs do. Saving lives is in their blood.

Suddenly Ann heard a loud bang, the crack of something broken down. In the fraction of a second, in her state of mind of shock, she was sure that she heard a devil with a shriek of laughter piercing her ears. Her head turned, the world whirled around, and she plunged herself into the black of nothingness – she lost consciousness. When she came to herself, one thought hurriedly came to her mind:

"Where's everybody? They all escaped. They are in

town. I have to find them!" She raised up in desperation and the adrenaline gave her new energy. Nothing was important anymore. Only one thing left to hope for. To see them again. She started to run toward the small town, Gradimir, without looking back.

In 1933, Ann was 16 years of age. She was arrested and sent to Siberia, to a Concentration Camp, the worst time during the Stalin 1930-1940. The nation was controlled by fear. She knew that she was going to a white hell in the snow of Siberia. She worked in the diamond minds, near the town of Mirny in the far east.

In the year of 1938, she escaped. It took her 3 years to get to Kiev, to make 6000 miles. She traveled by boat or truck or walked 15 KM a day. She could travel only in the summertime. She had to stop for the winter.

In the spring, she headed northeast, toward Ukraine. In 1941, during the early fall, she came to Kiev. She could not recognize the Russia she left several years ago. Now it was occupied by Germans. They were every-where. She quickly left Kiev and went to Gradimir.

CHAPTER 3

WHEN I CAME TO THIS WORLD

One day, in 1943, in the middle of April on an early Monday morning, Ann went to town. The day was sunny, and she took a walk and then she saw a crowd of people standing on the street. She was curious and joined the crowd.

She asked, "What is happening?"

"Take a look." To her surprise, she saw people walking in a line, escorted by German soldiers with big German Shepherd dogs.

Ann asked, "Who are they?"

Somebody answered, "They are Jews. It's a Jewish pogrom. They will be sent to the concentration camp and killed."

"Why?"

"Because they are Jewish."

Ann could not comprehend that. She just stood there with a very bad feeling in her heart. She noticed one woman from the Jewish group enveloping a baby in her arms. She was cuddling a child to herself. That child was me. Emilia. I had no awareness of being born just two months ago. I just was. I was everlasting – motionless. I had no notion of time without things being named – it felt good to exist.

I rested in my mother's arms, warm in the dark, peaceful, with the assuring heartbeat of my mother. Suddenly, abruptly, cold slammed into my face. At the same time, sharp light struck my eyes, blinding me. This brightness caused me to panic. Something pulled me up into the air. The blow was gusty, and in a fraction of a second, I was moving through the air and falling down. And then I felt warmth again, safe, with the heartbeat of my mother. Everything happened so fast that I didn't even have time to cry or make a noise. I could hear my mother's heartbeat again, but it was fast, like I had never heard before. I did not realize that I now had a new mother. (This is my imagination of what a baby could feel.)

My birth mother took advantage of the Germans not paying attention and threw me to the crowd. The one that caught me up was Ann, now my new mother. She pressed me close to her breast and ran to her apartment while my parents were marching away, never to be seen again. Ann never even knew their names. I never knew their names.

Ann murmured to herself, "I am not alone anymore.

I am not alone anymore. This baby must be 2 months old."

Ann made the decision that she must not stay in Russia, but she would go to Poland. From Kiev to Poland was not very far. She could walk there with the baby and her father. She knew the Ukrainian language and how to pray orthodox, so she could prove she was not a stranger.

The time was dangerous, no matter which way she would go, but she was full of hope, never giving up. She loved her new baby like her own. She went to the west of Poland, the city of Poznan.

After peace came to Poland, and the war was over, Ann was given a house in 1945. Because she had kept her land papers from communist Ukraine, she was able to receive this property within the communist system of Poland. The house was in the countryside with some land. It was a small farm. Now she could breathe fresh air, looking forward.

CHAPTER 4

MY FIRST MEMORY

My first memory started from visual experience. I was in a state of unconsciousness, in a world without shape, noiseless, weightless. I was in suspension, without the past, present or future. I emerged from gray existence. My brain awoke when I was passing through the door opening. I did not remember to open the door. I was like a shadow myself, like a spirit without touching anything. I entered a cube, a space, like in a box, a room – it was still, dark, gray. In the corner of my eyes, I saw black shadows of shapes, kitchen furniture, but I did not pay any attention to them.

Before me was a window with a bright light. I was attracted to the light like a moth. I moved silently toward it. When I stopped before the widow, I noticed that something was sticking to the glass. It was white. Pure white and incredible in shapes. There were many of these things. I looked closer and I was marveled. I had never seen anything like this before.

They were snowflakes, but I could not name them. I stood closer by the window and started to study them closely. These little stars covered the entire window. I saw them clearly – to me, they were big. They were designed masterfully, rich in shapes, fine and subtle, with great detail. They had arms stretched out from the center with perfectly straight, pure, white lines. Each branch line had small diagonal lines creating ornamentation. This decoration was a mystery to me and so incredibly beautiful that I was just delighted with it.

I didn't use all these words at the time. I am using them now to describe the snowflakes I saw then. I just took it by instinct. I could not stop watching them. Suddenly, I heard a noise. Behind the door I heard footsteps. I knew instantly it was my Grandpapa. I felt my face smiling, and I ran to the door. He brushed his boots from the snow. He opened the door and I saw his sweet, smiling face. He approached me, took off his gloves, and I saw a piece of candy in his hand. He gave me the candy. It wasn't wrapped in any paper, and I put it in my mouth. I do not remember the color of the candy, not even the taste, but I remember my own feeling of total happiness.

I do not remember how old I was at the time, but I was able to walk and even run. I also don't remember the tragedy of his disappearance. I was sleeping in his bed and suddenly I was alone in bed. I could not sleep, and I cried for a long time. Perhaps that is the reason for my phobia of loneliness, even today.

Later I was told that he was driving a wooden wagon that was pulled by a horse, going through the forest. At that time Poland was already a communist country, but the nation was divided into two groups. There were those accepting the communism, called "Reds", and those against communism, called "Whites". Whites were often hiding in the forests. They became partisans. When Grandpa was passing near them, he was stopped by them. Maybe he witnessed something he should not have, or maybe they did not like his Russian accent – for them he was probably Red. Whatever the reason, they murdered him. Ann cried for many years to come. She could never talk about him without tears.

CHAPTER 5

MY FIRST DRAWING

I grew up to become a healthy, happy girl. In my mind, I came from nowhere. One room was the universe. I had no idea if something existed beyond the walls. After a while, the room became a yard, the street, the town, the countries, the earth. With a poetic mind, I was going to travel to the stars and beyond. But for now, maybe in my 3-4 years of age, I was fascinated by the meadow before our farm. The grass was medium tall, full of flowers; white daisies dominating, but also red poppies and deep bluebottle were plentiful,

I was running through the field of colors, chasing the butterflies, and bees. Once I caught the bee and she stung me. That was a learning experience. I liked to hold little frogs in my hands and examine them. One morning a funny noise woke me up. My mom had just brought a little piglet to my bed. She stayed with me for a while. She was very, very pleasant. But what I liked the most was to watch the storks.

Facing our house was a barn and storks would come to the barn every spring. There were two of them and I watched them for days. They were big, bigger than chickens, walking across the top to the roof with their long legs, slowly, like in a slow dance. They were majestic. I watched how they made a huge nest, raising the little stork chicks, feeding them most of the time, living next to us like neighbors.

One day, as it turned into fall, they disappeared. I could not accept that. I could not forget them. I missed them. Impulsively, I grabbed an old, big nail and scratched their image on the hardcover of an old book. The cover was black, and the lines were white. I drew them spontaneously, in a hurry to have them again. The image was simplified, like intuitively creating symbols, foreshorten lines. I didn't realize it was a memory translated into a drawing. It looked like this:

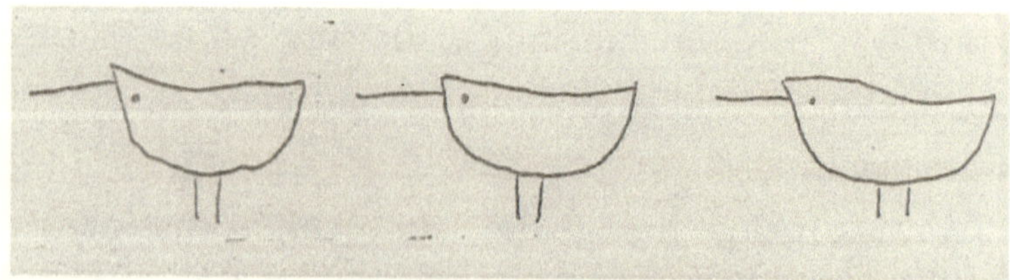

Since that day, I continued to draw on the book, on the paper, on the floor, in the dirt, in the sandy road with a stick, and any possible surface. Drawing became my language, naturally.

His Early Drawing

On the other side of the country, in the southern part of Poland, Zbigniew, the son of Joseph Fitz, made his first drawing, early in his age. I was never told exactly how old he was. Once, he became very ill, having a very high temperature for a few days. In this state, he had a terribly scary vision. He was in his bed when there was a big monster, half worm and half cockroach in his room. It was so real that he could not forget it. This experience was so strong that he had a need to talk about it to his parents. They did not believe him. They said he had hallucinated, and it was not real. But he was convinced it was real, so he wanted to prove that it was truth. He found another way to tell them his story. He made a very detailed drawing and showed it to his mother. It made a strong impression on her and she realized that he had really seen this monster. Zbigniew was growing up, busy with drawing all the time, which was natural to him.

White paper and black pencil were his choice. His drawing capacity became a strong tool of communication. Whenever he could not convince somebody, or explain something, he would draw. Others were impressed, often becoming his friends and that encouraged him to stay on this path.

CHAPTER 6

FEAR

I was never alone. My mom was always home. I loved her dearly. I had no idea that she was my stepmother. Even if I knew, it would not have made any difference anyway. I was too young to understand.

I liked to go outside, to the courtyard, all flat, spacious, with a threshing floor, without any grass. One day, I had gotten curious as to what was behind the barn. I went under the bush and squatted to see what was shining. It was just a drop of water, a dew. I stood up, and I found myself in a garden full of shrubs. I had never seen them before. They were imposing and dark. Suddenly, I felt strange. I just realized that I was a total stranger in this place. It was all unfamiliar, and I was totally lonely in this silence. I shuddered. "What's behind these dark things? What should I expect? What kind of creatures could hide there? Is it bad? Dangerous?" A great fear of the unknown came upon me. I turned my back quickly and ran home. I never went there again.

One day my parents left me home alone. They had never done that before. I was alone in total silence. What had been familiar now became strange. I could not recognize the white walls of the room to which I had not paid any attention before. The stillness of these white walls was not friendly.

"Why am I alone? What is in these empty walls?" I shuddered with chill. I was in terror. I started to call, "Mom! Mom!" – but nobody was home. My eyes got wider and wider. I started to cry. I was crying out loud. I was in a panic. I did not hear anything, but saw the walls starting to split. They were breaking. I saw the walls opening, and they kept breaking. I saw a black hole in it, and it got bigger and bigger. I was screaming and screaming and screaming…

I stopped only when I saw the door open, and my mom was there, coming. I never wanted to be alone again. Never, ever…never, never, never! I don't remember how old I was, but this feeling of the fear of loneliness stayed with me for life.

CHAPTER 7

MOLESTED

We had a big barn, the place to keep hay. It was filled very high with hay. I saw one ladder next to the haystack. I could never climb up by myself. One day I realized that I was on top of the haystack with my stepfather. He lay on his side next to me, and I was on my side also, facing him. He ordered me not to tell anything to my mom. I do not remember what he did to me, all I remember was my feeling of not liking it at all. And of course, I could never keep the secret from my mom. Whatever it was that he did, I told her about it right away. And then I heard her yelling at him very loudly behind closed doors. Since that day he changed. He hated me. He would yell at me or grumble and never stopped giving me hateful looks or cursing or calling me names. He never took me to the barn again, but later, much later, I understood what it was that happened.

Once, he wanted to check out the horse's hooves and ordered the horse to stand still. But the horse was not able to do it. So, he got angry, grabbed the shovel and struck the horse's belly. The horse screamed out. He continued to beat the horse over and over, and the horse kept crying out loud. I ran home to tell this to my mom, so she went outside to see what was happening. Another time he was repairing something. He wanted me to help him, to give him the nails one by one. But when I was not fast enough, he punched my cheek with the nail nipper. I did not cry. I just ran to my mom.

It was a beautiful summer morning. I went outside to play with the chickens. I checked the courtyard to see if there were any Jackdaws – they liked to steal little chicks. I looked around, and I noticed the chickens were near the barn. I do not know what kind of imagination I had at that time as a 4-year-old. I cornered one of the chickens and caught her. She was cackling in my hands as I went toward the well, in the middle of the courtyard.

I stopped at the well and started to push her down, "Go to the well", but she refused. She was beating her wings and screamed out. I got irritated and pushed her harder. I saw mom coming out from the house. At the same time my stepfather came from the other side of the yard. When he saw what I was about to do, he ran very fast toward me and before I could realize what was about to happen, something happened in a fraction of a second.

With his heavy boot he kicked me so strongly that I went flying in the air like a ball toward mom. When I fell and hit the ground, I lost consciousness. From then on, I was afraid of him. Children do not judge. They just remember their own feelings – fear. They only wish to escape, like a bird flying away when they see you approaching.

CHAPTER 8
BETWEEN ANGEL AND DEVIL

Since my stepfather was angry most of the time, Ann got an idea; "Maybe he doesn't like to work on a farm." She kept the documents about owning the farm in Ukraine. She went on to the City Hall asking if she could give back a farm and get something else in a different part of the country. Her request was accepted.

We moved to a new place, north of Poland, to a small town called Trzebiatow. At the end of town, there were houses built by Germans during the occupation. When they left, Polish people received these houses. It was a big one-story house with one acre of land. It was like a paradise. On the back of the house was an orchard. Apple trees, pears, plums and sweet cherries. On the right side of the house were two big trees of sour cherries. They were the best. When they were ready to eat, they were strong in taste, acid mix. With very, very much sweetness, so dark, almost black. I would climb this tree and eat until full. Imagine an orchard in bloom – it is heavenly.

At the front of the house were the most beautiful flowers in bloom from spring throughout the summer. The summer temperature was mostly 70 degrees – perfect for plants and humans. Flowers created a real carpet of colors, from yellow daffodils to red tulips. June was for Delphiniums – deep blue and they were taller than me. Next came huge flowers of Dahlias. Lilies stood peacefully, and peony buds ready to open. Roses were everywhere. All these colors attracted butterflies. In this paradise, mom was my angel. She would cuddle me close to her chest and whisper, "I love you baby. Promise you'll never leave me." So, I promised, genuinely. I liked the sound of her perfect heartbeat.

She was my angel until 3:00pm each day. At 3:00pm my stepfather would come home from work. I don't know what kind of work he had, but he got only 500 zloty a month, a very low income, not enough to buy meat. Most of the time we had soup with lard, onions, potatoes and bread. He was angry most of the time. But mom could buy 10 grams of sausage for me a day.

When I heard his footsteps behind the door, I said; "Mom, Devil is coming."

Ann answered, "Don't talk like this. Call him Dad – it may melt his heart."

"Mom, I tried that. Nothing works with him." Abruptly the door opened. He stood there looking angry, with a twisted face, mouth drawn. He was growling, and his eyes were red.

"I am working hard for you useless and this bastard, misbegotten. I am hungry, what do you do with the money?" He made a few steps into the room and stopped with eyes wide open. "What's this?"

"It's meat. A sausage on the table."

He roared, "Ah ha! See!"

Mom said softly, "It's for her. She's a child. She needs to grow."

He got mad like an animal, a beast. He threw the sausage to the garbage. He approached mom quickly and violently. He slapped her in the face with an open hand. She swayed but did not lose her balance. He kept hitting her. I was terrified! I ran toward him and with my little hands started to slap him repeatedly until he stopped.

Mom was pale and whispered, "Now, I'll leave you."

He was growling, "If you do that, I'll kill you both."

The next day she was weak and groggy with a black and blue face and frowned all day long without talking much. When he came home he was silent too. He felt it was not a day like every other day. When he sat down she came to him. "I need to talk to you. You could kill me. Since I cannot leave you, I have a different solution. If ever you do this again, I'll kill you. I can poison you, or even better, you sleep very deeply – I'll simply kill you while you're asleep. Remember, if ever you do this again, you will never have good sleep again."

He never got physical again, but he was brutal with his voice, unhappy, angry and hateful. I kept thinking, "He must be a devil."

I did not like anybody using strong language. Mom was very loving. She kept giving me my daily ten grams of sausage. But she was a strong disciplinarian. I had to ask her permission to do anything, even go to the toilet, which was outside in a big storage shed. I was very obedient, with respect for adults, never talking back. If ever I did something wrong, I knew I would be punished. She always kept a birch rod ready to correct me. She had rarely the reason to use it, because I was afraid of it. It would leave bruises on my legs, dark blue and dark red. But it happened only about once a year. I was not afraid of her. I knew she had a reason to punish me. However, I was afraid of my stepfather. I almost stopped talking. If somebody came to visit us, they would usually ask Ann if I were mute. "No, she's just shy," Ann would reply.

People were telling us that America was sending donations of food. We received one of these packages. It had one big orange in it. My parents gave me my portion of the orange, but I liked it so much that they gave me the rest – even him, my stepfather. I could not forget the taste of it for a long time. Strong, juicy and aromatic.

One summer day we were all outside. The moon had already come. It was a full moon. I looked at it and asked, "Why don't I see it during the day?"

Mom answered, "it's on the other side of the earth."

"What's on the other side?" I insisted.

"It's America."

"What's America?"

"It's a place where you can buy as many oranges as you want."

I paused and slowly said, "One day I have to see America. I have to see it." I was 7 years old. I could never think that was a premonition.

CHAPTER 9
GROWING UP

One day in 1953, when I was 10 years old, I came home from school and cried. "What's happened?" Mom asked.

"Stalin died. I was told at school that he was such a good man, gentle like a grandfather."

Mom sighed, "Now, I need to tell you the truth. Don't believe everything they tell you – it is communist propaganda. I was living in Russia under Stalin. He sent me to Siberia. I lost all my family. He killed millions of people." I believed her. But there was no peace at home. My step-father was grouchy, growling and hateful. It changed my mom. She lost patience. When they disputed, she yelled with a high-pitched voice.

When I got to be 12 years of age, I started to dream about the prince saving me, taking me from this home. I pictured him as a good, gentle person, very handsome and intelligent. When I reached my 13th year of age, I started to question if God existed – that would be good. If He did exist, I was sure science would discover Him one day in a laboratory. When I heard thunder, I thought, "If God exists, that could be His voice – but I am not afraid of the Life Giver."

When I was 14 years old, I lived in Lublin, east of Poland. I was liked at school because I could draw – so I was smiling at everybody. One day I saw the movie, "Lust for Life" which in Polish was called, "Passion for Life." Kirk Douglas portrayed Vincent Van Gogh. I was so incredibly moved that on my way home, a walk of two miles through the city, I was crying. I was moved by his passion and devotion. I looked at the sky like I was looking to the future. I felt something important had just happened – that I was called to become a painter, to be part of something extraordinary. I made a promise to myself to become a great artist, it simply felt right.

Somewhere in another part of Poland, Zbigniew Fitz, son of Joseph Fitz, had a similar experience. I had no idea about his existence but would learn about him later. He had already read Carol Stone's book about Van Gogh and his letters to Teo, his brother. He already admired Van Gogh. He knew that nothing was more important than being a painter. Every pain and obstacle would be worth passing through.

My mom wanted me to become a dressmaker. "You're always going to have a job," she said. But my dream was to be a painter. When I was 14 years old, I applied to the Art High School, secretly, and attended there from 1957-1962.

I was fascinated by Michel Angelo, a Renaissance genius. I wanted to learn to draw, so I brought the life model to school that everybody could study. When she got naked, most of the fellows were laughing so much that the teacher canceled the model. They were too young. I asked my mom to be my model, and she accepted.

I had lots of patience and a good sense of observance. I learned a lot and was grateful. I did not have any interest in boys. One of them said, "she's going to be a good wife." Other girls were fooling around.

I remembered a warning from my mom. "Remember, boys have only one thing in mind. They want to grab you to bed for a one-night stand."

In 1962, I finished high school. During vacation time, I got a job, got just enough to buy a train ticket to Cracow, to go to the Fine Art Academy. Without telling them about my plan, I left a note and escaped from home. I was already 19 years old.

CHAPTER 10

IF EVER I'LL MEET THE PRINCE?

I arrived in Cracow at the end of August – too late for the entrance examinations. I could only attend the Academy as a free listener. I found a roommate. We rented one room and shared the bed. I could not manage without help from mom, so I sent a letter to beg for money. She paid the rent and sent me a big piece of smoked lard, which I could keep for a long time.

As a free listener, I did not qualify for the mess hall. I could only steal a few slices of bread, and the soup was for free without anyone checking, so I could survive. When September came, I chose the studio of Professor Przebindowski. He gave the students a lot of freedom without imposing his own tastes. The next year, I passed the entrance examination. We all had to paint a still life. The board of examiners had to be impressed, because I was admitted to the 2nd year. Schools in Poland were tuition free. I changed the professor to Professor Rzepinski, hoping to learn more. He did not give much free-dom. He believed in Post Impressionism style.

In the basement of the Academy was a dance club. I didn't dance much before, but I decided to go. It was crowded. I walked around and went to the other room with tables to sit. I stopped in the entry and looked around. On my right was one boy, alone. He sat sipping a glass of wine. I looked at him, and he looked at me. I did something I did not think I should. I stood staring at him for several seconds. His big, dark eyes hypnotized me.

I felt shameful, so I turned my back and left the room. But he got up and followed me. He invited me to dance, and I followed his steps. It was surprising to me, but during the whole dance, he did not say a word. When the music ended, we sat down on the bench and after a minute or so he turned toward me, took my hand gently and said, "I need to ask you something. Promise me that from now on you'll never dance with anybody else."

While asking this, he looked deep into my eyes. His deep, dark mahogany, brown eyes were big and mesmerizing. He had an incredibly beautiful face. I do not know what happened to me, but without thinking at all I said, "Yes, ok."

He asked, "What's your name?'

"Emilia. And yours?"

"I am Zbigniew Fitz."

"Oh! I prefer your last name."

"Ok. You can call me Fitz." he answered, smiling.

I came to my room and remained shocked. I stood before the mirror and examined myself asking, "What could he see in me?" I was too short to have great sex appeal. I was petite, slim, brunette with a round face, childlike. My eyes were dark, big and almond shaped. "Maybe he was joking. Maybe he was drunk, but I didn't smell alcohol." I shuddered. Something in me told me that maybe…maybe…my life will change.

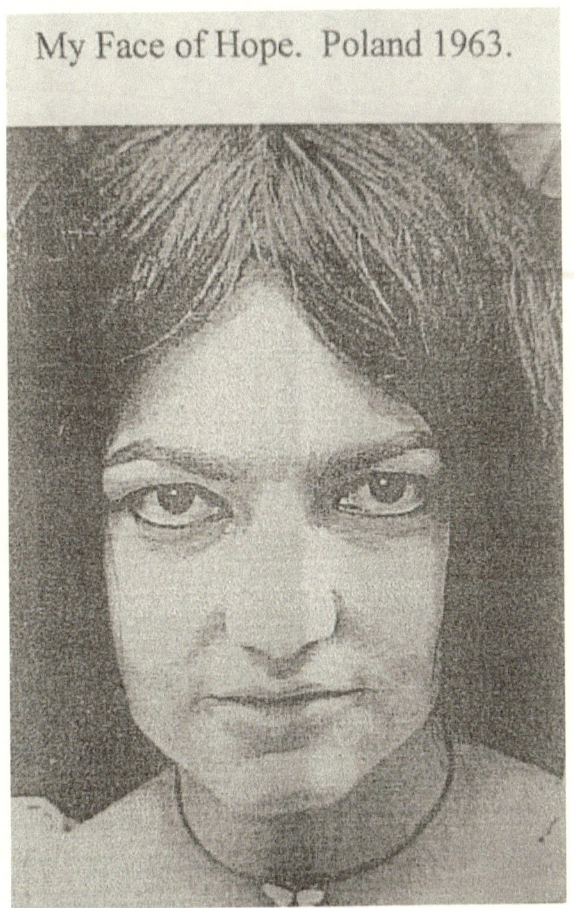

My Face of Hope. Poland 1963.

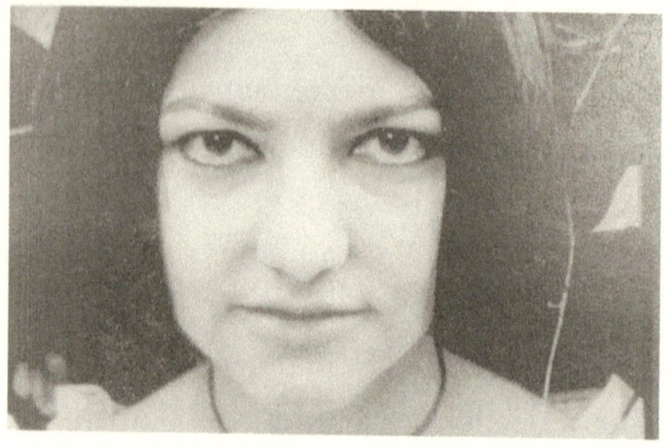

CHAPTER 11

FROM THE NEXT DAY ON…

The next day I went to the studio at The Fine Art Academy. Sometime later, one fellow approached me and asked, "a group of friends are going to the opera tonight. Would you like to go with us?"

"Sure," I answered.

He smiled, "Great! See you at 7:00 pm at the entry of the Academy." When I turned my back, he added, "and Fitz will be there."

I was a little surprised. I came at 7:00 pm. Fitz was there. Alone. Nobody else came. I asked, "Where is everybody?"

He said, "I don't know. They just didn't come. I hope you don't mind if we'll go to the opera anyway?"

"That's ok." What else could I say? I don't remember what the piece of work at the opera was. It was an instrumental, no voices raised in concert. The best part I liked was the string orchestra; the chorus of violins created a heavenly sound. I didn't know much about classical music, but this time this sound penetrated my soul – it was soothing.

When we left the opera, it was already dark. We walked in the city lights, slowly toward my room. Everything was in the center of the city, within a short distance. We talked and questioned each other. I learned that he went to the same kind of fine arts high school. He had a good teacher, Adam Hoffman, who kept telling him, "remember, not a day without a stroke. You need to draw every day."

Time went fast, and we were at my door. He asked, "when can I see you again?"

I paused. "I don't know."

He quickly added, "How about tomorrow, after classes? Meet me at 5:00 pm at the fountain next to the Mariachi Church at the plaza."

"Ok"

"So, see you tomorrow. Goodbye."

And he left. I was surprised and impressed. I thought, "How about that? He didn't kiss me. He didn't even try! A real gentleman." He was tricky with this date, but he treats me with respect. But I must be careful. He's smart. I must remember the warning of my mom. And he's so handsome. It will be hard to say "no."

CHAPTER 12

NO STOLEN KISS

We met at the fountain each day at 5:00pm. We needed to learn about each other, so we had lots of questions. I asked, "Who is your master painter?"

He answered, "Van Gogh."

I was pleased. "Me too! I liked his passion after I saw a movie about him."

"I liked him before the movie," Fitz added. "I read the books about him. Do you know that Van Gogh never sold any paintings, but he painted anyway?"

"When art is your calling," I replied, "you don't think about money."

Fitz nodded. "Yes, it is in you. You must do it. It is about your conscience. To be truthful to yourself is to be truthful in art. That will give the quality."

I paused, "And originality, because everybody is different."

He smiled tenderly. "Together we can become great artists."

"What else can you tell me about yourself?" I asked. He stopped to think for a moment.

"I like to read. I read a lot. Classical literature. Dostojewski. I have also liked to take photos since I was 10 years old."

Then another question came to my mind. "What colors do you like?"

He answered quickly. "Black. And you?

"I like ultramarine and deep red. Why do you like black?"

He frowned. "I think it has something to do with my first memory. It was the end of WWII. I was probably 2 years old and I remember we were hiding in a cellar. My mom had a candle. It was dark, but the light from the candle was the same as what Rembrandt painted, so I like him too."

The next question was important to me. "What do you like about me?"

He smiled. "I like your big eyes. I feel there's more in them. I like your innocence. And your passion for art. I have never talked about art with other girls."

After several dates he felt the time for a kiss had come. When I said, "Goodbye" he pressed a quick kiss to my cheek. When he tried to kiss my lips, I moved away. "No. It is too soon." He tried again and again, but I had my trick. I bowed my head and laid it on his chest, so he could only kiss the top of my head. It wasn't easy for me. His smell had a strong effect on me. It ignited a desire.

Then he said, "I am going to steal the kiss."

I answered, "I will be vigilant." And then I added, "But if you ever force me for anything, I'll never see you again."

He stopped, "No. It is not in my character. I'll never force you for anything."

I smiled and left. That night I couldn't sleep. How many girls would accept anything he wanted. I didn't want to be easy. I needed to test him. If he didn't care enough for me, then he would walk away. But I needed his respect and to be sure I could trust him.

We were very compatible, and when I would see him, it would make me melt. But I needed to be strong and resist his advances. Was I in love? I felt it from the first moment I met him. Was I falling in love?

CHAPTER 13

JOKE THAT COULD DESTROY ALL

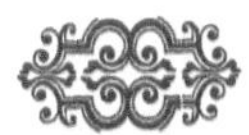

Everyday we met at the fountain. Usually I was late, and I was running through the streets, but when I saw him from the distance, I slowed down, pretending to just walk slowly. When I arrived, I was panting and breathless, desperately trying to hide that. But he had this smirk on his face, probably he saw me running but never said anything. I also saw him smoking cigarettes. I asked him if he smoked a lot. He said, "I have been smoking since I was 10 or 11 years old." I began to understand that his smell that was attractive to me was coming from the cigarettes. I had never smoked, so I did not recognize the smell, but it did not change anything. I was already attracted to him, only I did not want him to know that. I did not want to be vulnerable.

"Do you like coffee?" he asked.

"Yes."

"There's a nice coffee shop nearby. We can go there and sit and talk."

"Ok."

We sat down at the table, used lots of sugar in our coffee and drank sip by sip, slowly. I finally broke the silence. "I saw your drawings at Academy. They are very skilled."

"Yes," he said. "You need to study from a live model. Observe bodies in action, not only static, but foreshorten, short cuts like in perspective."

I nodded. "I know. That's what Michelangelo did."

He continued, "if you study regularly, you will memorize, and after years of practice, you will be able to do your own vision even without using models."

I nodded again, "You are right. If an artist does not study, you can see inadequacy in his images."

He paused, "I need to ask you something. This afternoon a few of my friends are going on a short trip to the River Vistula, not far from the city. Would you like to go?"

"Sure," I replied.

He stopped at his home and said, "wait 2 minutes." He came out quickly with 2 sandwiches, bread and a few slices of sausage.

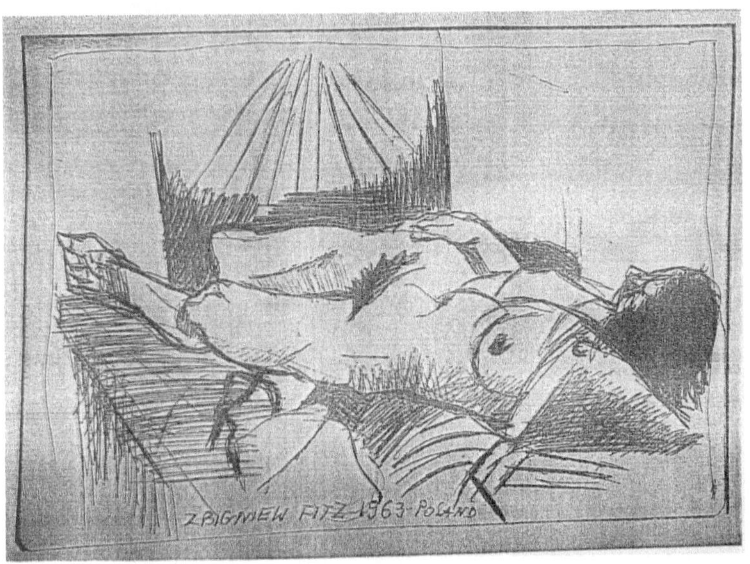

I was very excited. I did not know his friends, two boys and one girl. After a quick introduction, they were anxious to go. We arrived at the Vistula River. It was very wide and calm. It was idyllic. Water ran in slow motion, dull in color, amber-dark, dirty green – it felt deep. The field around was grassy with grass-hoppers singing. Along the slope forget-me-nots reflected the blue sky. Other purple and yellow flowers were as spectacular as garden flowers. Dragonflies were flying, impossible to catch. But I caught a toad – when I covered her with my hands she was calm, safe, and I could feel cloth like skin.

His friends were telling funny stories, laughing and giggling while chasing the girl. When it was getting late, we approached a heavy metal bridge, wider than the river and very high above the river. We were in the middle of the bridge, and we stopped and looked down. I was a little afraid of that height. Suddenly, abruptly, before I could realize what just happened, I was caught and picked up. I saw myself above the river, outside of the bridge. I froze with terror. I almost stopped breathing. I closed my eyes and became motionless. I only heard a silent snicker, a choking laughter, and I knew that Fitz was hanging me over the river with a strong grip. When he finally put me down, I was so in shock, I did not say anything for a while.

He finally broke the silence, "Did you have fun?" At first, I did not say anything. I just gave him my angry look. He touched my arm.

I hissed, "This joke was not funny at all! You are unpredictable, and I cannot trust you. I do not want to see you again!" I started to walk toward my room, and I did not say anything anymore. He followed me and kept asking for forgiveness. I maintained a stony silence. I shot lightning from my eyes toward him. I was sulky, my eyes sparking with fury. Finally, we reached my door.

"I do not want to lose you," he said. "Man and woman should never be angry at each other. They were created to love one another. But I made a mistake with my stupid joke. Did I ruin everything? Can I see you tomorrow?"

I did not answer. I kept my sulky face. I turned my back and left, angrily.

CHAPTER 14
TORMENTED

I entered my room, and my stomach immediately tightened into knots. I kept my feelings of indignation. I collapsed on my bed and pressed my face into the pillow, sobbing.

"Is it over? Is it over?" I had to ask myself, "Do I really want that?" And I had to answer honestly. "He is everything I ever wanted. When I look at him, I forget I am lost. I melt when he heartily smiles at me. He is not only handsome, but gentle, polite, intelligent, educated and talented. We agree on almost everything."

And yesterday, he had said, "I don't want to lose you." It means he is serious about me, but if we are to stay together, I have to trust him. How can I trust him now, when he is so unpredictable? But if I reject him, I'll be unhappy for the rest of my life. The moment of truth came over me. I could not deny it anymore. In my heart, I knew I loved him. But after being so angry with him, I am not sure if he will ever approach me. Just the thought of losing him forever made me miserable and sobbing again. But if he will come to me, I have to find the way to test him. The trust is the most important thing in a relationship. In trust, love will grow. But what if he will not come to me? I'll be devastated. With that thought, I fell asleep.

I woke up early. I noticed that my roommate had not come home. I never questioned her about her private life. This time I was happy that she wasn't there to see my swollen eyes from sobbing. It was time to go to the Academy. When I came to the gate, I saw him waiting for me. He said, "Hiya" and I smiled. I was glad to see him and I didn't hide that. He looked at me and said, "You look tired."

I told the truth. "I was crying."

He was also sincere. "I could not sleep. I was worried if I ruined everything because of my stupid joke. I wanted to bring you flowers, but I have something better." He gave me a postcard with Van Gogh's *Sunflowers*. He wrote, "These are the most beautiful flowers that I know." It touched me so much that I could never forget it.

I looked closer at the flowers, and I noticed, "They are withered."

He replied, "Look how colorful they are."

"Why? If they are dying?" I asked.

"He answered, "Maybe he didn't believe in the total mortality of things."

And I added, "Yes, maybe it's a metaphor of his own beliefs."

He answered again, "Maybe, but it is beautiful."

I asked: "His beliefs?"

He paused. "Both. His beliefs and his execution. His talent."

I added, "And people feel that. That's why they love him so much."

He said slowly, "Even if he was a loser. He never sold anything. He wanted to be a priest. He chose art and believed in honesty in art."

"His devotion was touching."

We stopped at the entry of the Academy. He looked at me and smiling said, "We are such a perfect match."

I agreed, "Yes we are."

He added, "I didn't want to lose you."

I whispered, "Me too."

He asked, "Can I kiss you now?" I directed my forefinger to my forehead and closed my eyes. He kissed me on my forehead tenderly and said, "I'll never force you for anything." I gave him a gaze full of love, and each of us went to the studio with good feelings in our hearts.

CHAPTER 15

HIS PORTRAIT

It felt good to admit to myself that I loved this man. It was like a dream come true. When will the time come for our first kiss? It had to be a very special occasion. I ran to the fountain full of joy. When I came to him my first question was: "What if you had dropped me down from the bridge?"

He was laughing. "No way, my grip is so strong. I can squeeze the juice from a rock."

"Where did you get your strength?" I asked.

He paused. "Maybe because when I was a teenager, I worked on the railroad. I was also transporting milk. I had to load up the truck. Lifting milk cans was heavy work. The milk smelled too, so I do not like milk."

I smiled. "My mom sent me a smoked bacon with very little meat in it."

He asked, "Do you like it?"

I replied, "When you are hungry, you like anything."

The next day he brought me a dessert. "It is something I like, so I hope you will like it."

"What is it?"

"It's a Halvah."

"Oh! I like that." It was a big piece. I knew I would measure the portions to keep it if possible. When we wanted to go to the coffee shop, I asked, "Should we start to draw people?"

"Yeah, we will be quick on the draw."

"Let's go to buy a sketchbook." We had only enough money for one book, so we had to share. I wanted to start by drawing his portrait. Drawing his portrait gave me the opportunity to stare at him, to study not only the surface, but feel him as a person. He had a good appearance, was a man of noble bearing, with a perfect posture in admirable proportion.

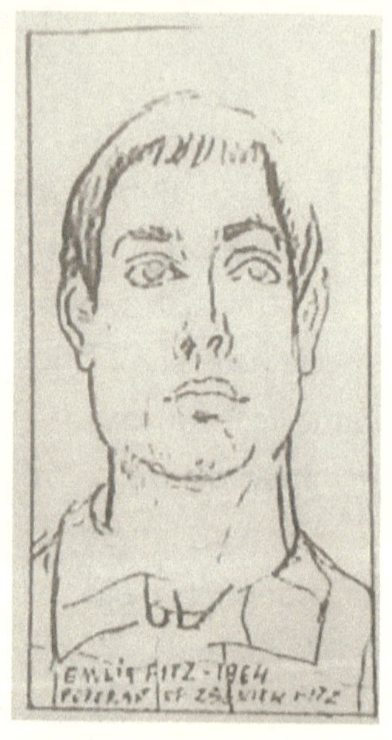

His face was so incredibly beautiful, like a divine, ancient classical Greek statue – all perfect: nose, lips, eyes, strong jaw, but warm, full of sympathy. He was a gentle man (always opening doors for me), tolerant, without judgement, but at the same time with strong opinions, especially about art. He believed in his natural talent, potential and need to be truthful to achieve great quality in art. He was a dreamer, wanted to fly high, to become a great artist, disinterestedly like Van Gogh. He believed in education, a high level of culture and professional honesty to achieve perfection – that was a responsibility. What a beautiful person. I could only look at him with admiration.

CHAPTER 16

FIRST KISS

Suddenly he asked teasingly, "When can I kiss you?"

I looked in his eyes amorously. "There will be a special occasion. I am going to go to Lublin to visit my parents for Christmas, and I am invited to a New Year's Eve party. I would like for you to come with me."

"Ok!" He answered with enthusiasm.

It was obvious that our destiny would be fulfilled. I liked the idea to kiss in public, just to feel safe. The big day came. I felt solemnly, my decision was made – he is going to kiss me. I had never been kissed before, but now he would be my prince. I was sensing that he was the one, for life. How do I know that? I just know.

Finally, we met. He was staring at me with admiration, and I was staring back at him. His deep, dark eyes were melting my heart. On our way to the party we didn't utter a single word and yet we felt like we said so much. The feeling of love is real, so pure in its glory. It will shine through our lifetime.

Before opening the door, he whispered, "I love you." I had no strength to react. I just pressed my head to his arm. We entered the room with loud music where everybody was dancing. On the left side of the room was a sofa. We sat down, and he held me close. Almost immediately, without a word, he started to kiss me.

The earth slipped from under my feet. I was totally submissive, absorbing him. The world disappeared. I wanted this kiss to last forever. It was not about the specifics of the kiss, but about the meaning. About our closeness. The kiss felt so close, like our souls were penetrating through each other, sharing everything we were. I felt him, his breath, his heartbeat. This feeling of closeness is indescribable. The joy, a different state of being, puts us in ecstasy, to share each other.

The kiss was a statement that from now on I'd never be alone. I sensed that I would never live by myself and for myself. One kiss wasn't enough. It was kiss after kiss, again and again. We wanted each other forever. We lost sense of time. We continued to kiss all night until morning.

We finally had to stop because everybody started to leave. We started to walk toward my home. I was feeling a little weak. I also felt my lips were very hot. I touched them and to my surprise, my lips were swollen. I asked him, "How do they look? What color?"

He smiled. "They are deep red and purple with a touch of deep blue."

My voice became fast. "Oh! My God, it's not funny. What will I tell them at home?"

He paused. "Tell them you fell down, and it was a bad fall."

When the time came to say goodbye, I said, "I'll come to Cracow in a week. I can't show myself like this."

He kissed me on the forehead. "I'll miss you."

I came home, and my mom shouted out, "What happened to you?"

"I fell down."

They looked at each other and bent their heads. It was clear they didn't believe me. Mom went outside to bring in snow. "You need a cold compress." She took a washcloth and wrapped the snow and applied it to my mouth for 10 minutes. It made my lips feel numb. She took the compress for about 15 minutes. She reapplied that a few times a day but the first day she used this on and off every 15 minutes. It took 3 days for the swelling to go down.

I couldn't stop thinking about him. I was melting just at the thought of kissing him again. But we'll not go any farther. I must build my strength. It would be against my convictions that I'll give myself totally to my prince. Only to my husband. That was the promise I made myself since a long time ago. But I sensed that he was going to be the one…

CHAPTER 17

OUR NIGHT IN THE WILDERNESS

One day we were walking through the streets toward my room. He wrapped his hand around my shoulder, bent his head close to my head and whispered in my ear, "Would you go with me on a trip during vacation time?"

"Where?" I asked.

"To the wilderness. To the mountains. Let's forget about the whole world. Just the two of us."

I was curious. "Which mountains?"

"To the most beautiful place, east of Poland, close to the Ukrainian border, Bieszczady."

I paused; I was surprised. "Let me think about it. I'll give you my answer tomorrow."

"Please say yes. It will be the trip of our life."

I went home thinking. "This idea is totally against my logic. If I consider, I must be crazy. I can ruin my life.

It is a great risk. But I cannot ignore my deep-seated feelings for the man of my life. But I need to trust him. I need to know if he can respect me. If I do not test him, I may regret it for the rest of my life. If he can respect me now, he will respect me later in life."

I was hesitant. I was torn between two feelings, totally tormented. What if he is a civilized, respectful, good man? That would be a unique treasure. I need to know. I am going to take the risk. I will tell him, "Yes" – is my instinct good?

The next day his first words were, "What is your decision?" I stopped without a word. He was impatient "Please, don't torture me?"

But first I wanted to remind him, "Remember, you said once that you will never force me to anything."

"Yes, I remember, and I want you to trust me."

I paused and slowly replied, "In this case, ok. I am going with you, to take a risk."

I saw this smirk on his face, like, "Ok, girl, we will see when we start to kiss." And he started to kiss me, tenderly.

After that he was excited and started to talk fast. "We need to prepare. We need a tent, two knapsacks, many packages of dry soup, a sewing box, blankets, an air mattress and air blower."

I was surprised. "Why do we need a sewing box?'

He replied, "The nights are cold. We will need to bring hay from nearby fields, sew it between two blankets and it will keep warmth very well."

When we arrived, we had to walk several miles. There were no houses, only some orchards, but deserted land, uninhabited. Something bad had happened here during WWII. "How do you know about this place," I asked.

He answered, "Years ago I came here with a boy-scout troop. There is a cabin at the top of the mountain, but I am sure it is closed." We had to climb the mountain. It was very steep. When I got tired, he gave me some cubes of sugar. Finally, we arrived at the top. It was breathtaking! After a short break we had to prepare for the night. When it was all ready, we kissed, but I was not relaxed. I prepared myself for this moment for many months. I wanted to be in control, stay alert and overcome my desire.

It started to get dark. We ate the soup with bread. We went inside the tent when it was dark. Inside it was pitch black. We could only feel each other and could not see anything. We lay down next to each other. I felt jittery, not knowing what his reaction would be to the surprise I had for him. I needed to be calm, but it is easier said than done.

He took me into his embrace and started to kiss me very slowly, more and more passionately. I was waiting for the next step and I was trembling at the thought of that moment. As soon as I felt his hand going down, I said, "No!" When he did not stop, I said again, "No, no, no, no!" I pushed him off me.

He stiffened, and I froze. It was total silence. There

was high tension between us. I was terrified. I did not know what to expect. Suddenly, he grabbed the flash light and enlightened his face. I heard his voice thick with emotion. "Look at my face." He was visibly deeply moved, shocked. I didn't say anything, just turned my back and pretended to go to sleep. I felt slightly panicked, but I also understood he was not going to force me to do anything I did not want. I felt assured and slowly calmed down. Peace came upon me.

In the morning I woke up happy, everything in me was smiling. I glanced at him furtively. He woke up before me but didn't say a word. He went out and prepared soup for us. We didn't say a word to each other for the next several hours. He took a walk, and I followed him. There were no trees on the top of the mountain. It was calm, no breeze and so beautiful. He broke the silence. "Why did you come with me?"

"I wanted to test you," I answered.

He paused. "Hmmm…I told you. I'll never force you to do anything."

I pressed my head to his chest, "Thank you. Now I can trust you." After a while, I had the question, "Do you still love me?"

He quickly replied, "Yes, I love you. More than ever. And I respected you for who you are before this trip."

I looked up to his face to meet his eyes. "With trust, our love will grow." He embraced me tenderly and wanted to kiss me, but I stopped him. "Wait, wait. We should not kiss here, because it may be hard for us."

He grinned. "You are right," and added with laughter, "kissing in public is better." We looked at each other with eyes full of love. Love is about feelings, and it is a taste of heaven.

CHAPTER 18

WHAT IS THE FUTURE?

We were waking up each morning with smiling faces, without pushing the future. Once I said, "Your mom raised you well."

He paused. "Good books raise me."

"How did you know which books were good?"

He paused again. "That had to come from my mom. She had a very strong sense of moral value."

In the next several days there were no more soups. We had money only for one loaf of bread. I came up with an idea to send a postcard to my mom and ask her to send us some food. I knew she would never say "No" if I were in need. So we went several miles to the nearby country village, sent the letter and waited a few days. We went again to see if there was any package for us. We went to the Post Office and to our surprise, my mom was sitting on a chair waiting for us.

She said, "I have bread and dry sausage for you." We

went to the tent. Climbing the mountain was very hard for mom. When we stopped, we were very hungry and couldn't wait for the sausage. She looked around and asked, "Where am I going to sleep? I see the cabin."

We said, "The cabin is empty, and it's closed."

I added, "I don't see any other choice. You have to sleep with us." We all went to the tent for the night. We got up early. It was very tight. We were all dreadfully cramped.

When we finished our breakfast, mom said, "my children, there's not enough food. We are cramped. I think we have no other choice. We need to go back home to Lublin. We knew she was right. We didn't protest. We packed quickly and left.

When we came home, after a short break, Mom suddenly asked Fitz, "Do you want to marry her?"

I interrupted, "Oh! No, mom no! Don't push him."

He interfered, "Stop! Emilia, stop! I want to marry you."

Mom looked at his face, "When?"

"As soon as possible," he replied.

Mom frowned, she was thinking. "Let's do the wedding in the middle or end of September."

"Ok" Fitz grinned.

Mom turned to me. "You have to go back to Cracow to your rented room. I am going to go to work. I must go to the countryside to be a traveling salesman. Ordering big photos and portraits from small photos can bring me good money. We will need it for your wedding."

Fitz asked, "Is it hard for you?"

Mom answered, "No, I just have to walk from door to door, from village to village. People give me food and a sleeping place. I have been doing this a long time. Don't worry. I'll be ok."

We came back to Cracow and I started to prepare. I had to make a wedding dress. I asked Fitz's mom if I could take curtains from her window. It was perfect; white, soft and transparent. I also needed a wire hanger to do the hat. I had to sew by hand, so it was time consuming. Time was passing fast. September was approaching. A new chapter of our life was coming, built on love and hope for the future.

CHAPTER 19
WEDDING

Time was shrinking fast. In agony of impatience, I counted the days: five…four…three…and only two left. I knew he was my prince, the love of my life. I could trust him because he proved himself, restrained his wildest desire when I was at his mercy in the wild and no one around.

He is so perfect on so many levels: handsome, righteous, gentle, strong, wise, noble. I sighed dreamily, and I shuddered involuntarily at the thought of our first night. But I was not nervous because of the trust. Finally, one day left!

I was ready. My hat went well with my dress. The only thing that was needed was a bouquet of white roses. I asked him to buy them. He went out and came back with a nice smile. But I couldn't believe what he brought. Instead of roses, it was a small bouquet of violets – about 3" x 5" in size. With eyes wide open I said, "I wanted roses."

He grinned. "But violets are pretty too, and they are cheap. Roses are much more expensive."

I grumbled, "I'm not going to the wedding with these flowers."

He asked, "Why?'

"Because it's too funny."

He stood in consternation. I was already angry, sulky. I shrugged and left the room. As I walked through the streets, I could see how impulsive I was. He was calm. I was thinking, "Now, what? Is my dream broken to pieces because of roses? Is he going to let me go away?"

That was our first misunderstanding. As I was walking, suddenly I felt him wrap his hands around my shoulder. "We are not going to destroy what's between us because of these stupid flowers. Come home. I'll buy you the white roses." He whispered, "I love you too much. I don't want to lose you."

He pushed me gently back to his apartment. In a short while, he brought me the most beautiful bouquet of white roses. I flung my arms around his neck and gave him a thank you kiss. After a while he said, "I need to tell you something."

"Yes?"

"I spoke with a priest. He needed some papers like a certificate of your baptism. Your mom said that she's not your real mom. She saved you during WWII because you are Jewish. She asked the priest not to tell you that."

I paused. "Now I understand why she didn't want me to look for my real father. Our small family of 3 people and each of us has a different name."

He added, "My mom is Polish. My father was Jewish."

I said, "I know. Your mom told me this story."

"He asked, "How do you feel? About your mom?"

I said, "To me, it makes no difference. She's the only mom I know, and I love her. Maybe I should be married in a synagogue, but I never saw any in Poland – all the churches are Catholic."

He grinned. "And I don't want to wait."

The next morning, we all went to church. The day was sunny, and I felt solemn. When the priest made me repeat the wedding words, I choked up with emotion. The new life had just begun, full of promises.

After the wedding ceremony, we all came back to the apartment with a small group of guests – only 10 people. One person was missing, Fitz's stepfather. His mom made him go away because he was an alcoholic. My parents brought goose meat to the celebration. It was delicious.

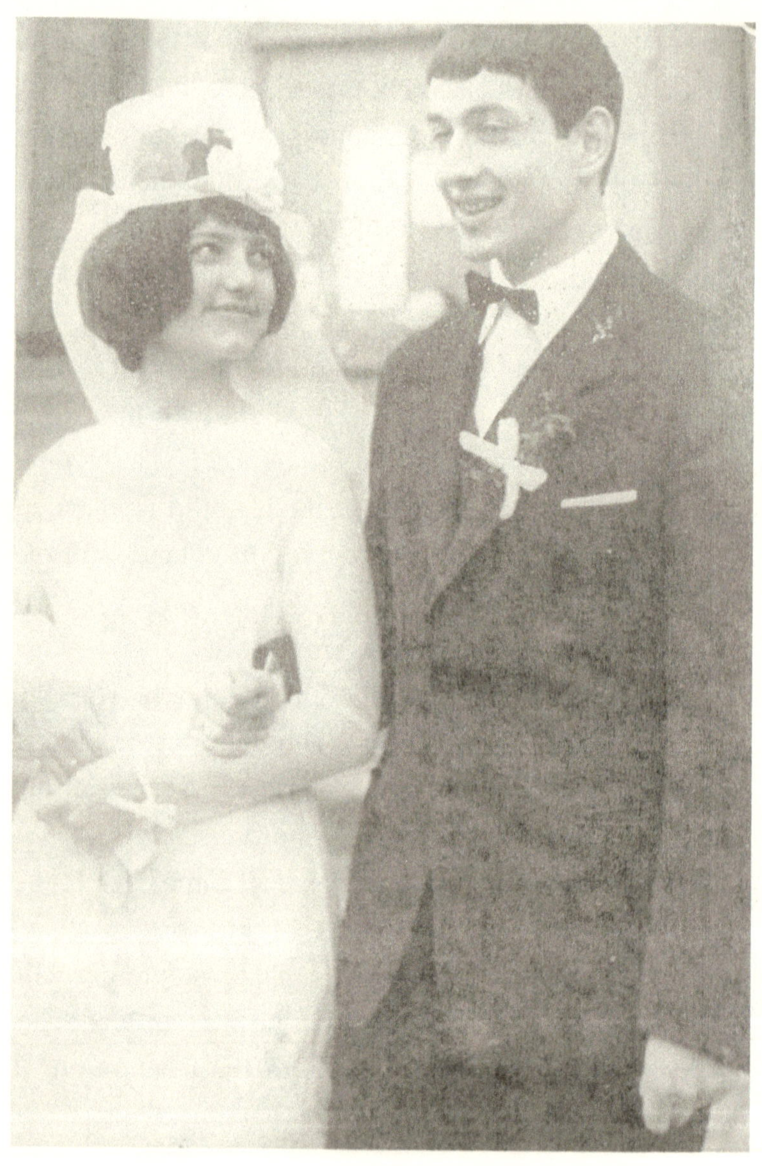

Our happiness after the wedding

CHAPTER 20

OUR FIRST NIGHT

Finally, we were alone, in the silence of our small room. Without a word, we were staring at each other, trying to penetrate our souls. He broke the silence. "Come here." He reached for me, pulling me closer to him. With his strong hands, with one sudden jerk my wedding dress was torn off. I did not regret the dress, because I made it myself, so it was for free. He picked me up and carried me to the bed, pulled me down and posed gently. I did not resist. I felt safe.

When he was next to me, he whispered, "You are mine forever."

I whispered back, "If we will love until death, our love will endure through eternity."

He replied, "If there is eternity."

I replied, "I wish there is."

There were no more words. We started to kiss like the first time, making me forget about the whole world. The enormous feeling of love was passing through all my being, like floating in heaven. Suddenly I was shaken, like the shock of a tornado. Sharp pain shot through me. I screamed, "Ow!" He stopped and just stared down at me. "What happened?" I left the bed in all consternation.

He threw open the sheet, and I heard his voice full of joy, "Blood stain."

I thought to myself, "Did he doubt me, if I were lying about my virginity? Now, he can trust me. I did not lie."

He said with sensitivity, "Don't worry, Baby. Everything will be o.k. Tomorrow I'll give you some aspirin. There will be no more pain. Now, come back to bed."

I calmed down, came back to bed, cuddled with him and went to sleep. I woke up a little nervous. I didn't talk too much. My husband showed me a lot of affection throughout the day, whispering lovingly, assuring and kissing gently.

Our second night approached. After our last meal he gave me some aspirin. "It's a miracle pill. It will make you happy." I grinned and felt hopeful. When we went to bed, he started to caress me very slowly until a jolt of attraction moved through my body. He felt my readiness pervaded by love. We sank into each other. There was no pain. The world disappeared. We became one. It felt right. I was at peace. This night of intimacy was a confirmation of the unity of our spirits, to complete our whole beings and sense of belonging. It was a fulfillment of our destiny.

CHAPTER 21

MY HEAVEN

People called us parrots – we were always together, holding hands. Both of us had Grant-in-Aid, so we could buy art materials. At the Academy, there were some students who liked vodka so much that they were selling their canvas to get more alcohol. We bought them.

One day we came home, and his step-father came at the same time. He was drunk. He swore, cursed and called me a whore. I went to the apartment, and the two of them stayed on the stairs. Suddenly I heard my husband, terribly agitated, talking fast. He probably smashed the drunkard to the wall with his iron hands. My gentle man became so angry that he scared the drunkard to death. From that day, he never said any bad words to me. He just stayed in his room, mumbling to himself when drunk.

The apartment was small, only two rooms. In our room was a big ceramic stove 7 feet high. Every day in the winter, a fire had to be prepared to burn coal. Everybody had their own cellar to keep coal. My mother-in-law, with the stepfather, lived in the kitchen. I remember my mother-in-law sitting on the bed with her cat, petting him. She was a very gentle, sweet person. I loved her like my mom, and she loved us. There was never any dispute in our home. I felt so comfortable with my husband that I became talkative, but he was rather reserved, thoughtful.

Each morning when we both woke up, there were two rolls with a sausage waiting for us. His mother would bring them without ever waking us up. In the springtime, she would bring a big bouquet of lilacs. She knew how much her son liked the smell of these flowers. I was so moved by this, that I started to love flowers, which would become my passion for life.

One day his mom asked me if I could cook dumplings. I said, "yes," but that was a lie. I went to the grocery store, where people were always in line, mostly women. I approached a woman and asked her how to make dumplings. I took a note of every word she said, went home and cooked. When everybody started to eat, I asked if they liked it and they all responded with "yes, they are very good." But when I started to eat them, I knew they were only being kind and did not want to hurt my feelings. I had no idea why my dumplings were hard to chew. I felt terrible. They never again asked me to cook anything.

My husband had a very nice jacket, which came from an American donation. It was a deep red but had started to fade. I wanted to do something good. I offered to turn the other side. I followed all the stitches, sewed them up together with all the needlework done by hand. It took me a long time. When it was ready, I gave him his jacket. To my horror, somehow the jacket was smaller – not much, but enough to make me feel bad.

One day I asked Fitz to stop smoking. He said, "I tried. It's too hard. I can't stop smoking." It made me angry.

I felt my face becoming sulky. "If you keep smoking, then I'm going to learn to smoke too!" I grabbed the cigarettes and the matches, went to the open window and tried to light up a cigarette. I had never smoked before. But before I could do that, he brusquely jumped toward me, pulled the cigarette from my hand and threw it out the window. I could see he cared about me.

He said, "don't you ever make the same mistake I did." I was moved. I hugged myself to his chest and we kissed, endearingly.

I thought, "If heaven exists, it must be full of love." Image of heaven is not about things in it, but about feelings. Since I had married, I was in a blissful state. Our apartment was a little heaven on earth. He is my heaven.

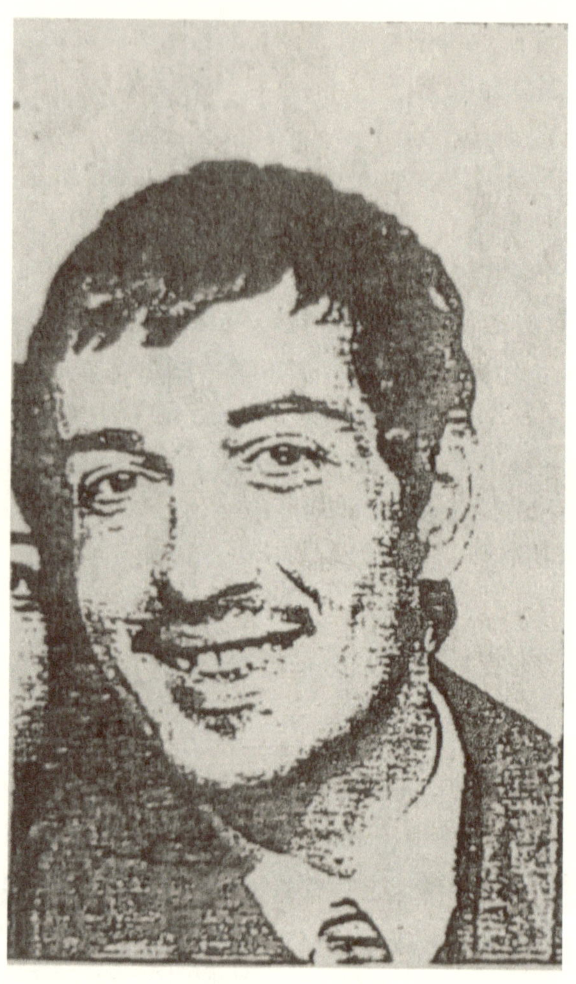

He had a nice smile, and I loved him to death.

CHAPTER 22

NOT A BACHELOR ANY MORE

In the spring of 1964, Fitz, along with two friends, Mark W. and George M., got jobs as night guards at the National Museum in Cracow. They had many long nights to have discussions about art. They created a manifesto and group "A." Later there were 7 members. I was the only woman in the group. Their slogan was, "Ball is Round," to be straight forward in creation. Aizm meant indifference about problems of styles. Formal problems are not enough to create the painting. Image is not a copy of reality, but the opinion about it. Image is not only a reflection of optical perception. Content creates a form. They kept exhibiting with forums.

At academy, we continued to do post impressionism, where everybody painted in spotty specks, colorful and twinkling. There was no artist's personality, all was studio made, like it was by the same person. When we came to our apartment, we painted figuratively, trying to learn the basics. We also studied styles. One day, Fitz sat at the table going through the art book. I was watching his beautiful face, and I wanted to pinch myself again and again to believe that this man was my husband.

One image from the book caught my attentionit was impressionist French painter, Claude Monet. He painted the garden. I already loved flowers. It was a dream garden, shimmering with colors. Nothing was precise, so I could use my imagination.

Everything was fleeting and made me wish to go inside of this painting. I said, "I wish to have a garden like this one day."

He grinned. "I'll try to make your dream come true."

I caressed his head with love-kindness.

The city of Cracow gave Group "A" a room, rent free, which they could use to paint or meet. It was a very small room, but they were happy about it. It was very close to our apartment, on a parallel street. My husband went there for a few minutes. When he came back after one hour, I asked him not to go without me. He said, "Yes, yes," but didn't really mean it. The next day he went to buy cigarettes and came back after 2 hours.

When he came back, I was very angry. "I know you went to the studio. You are not a bachelor any more. We have the same profession, no children, accept that."

He said, "I'm sorry."

I asked, "Why are you going without me?"

"Because they don't want you to go there."

"Why?"

"Because they bring girls to sleep with them, and they don't want you to see this."

That made me even more angry. "I don't want to talk with you anymore. If you go there again without me, that may be the end of our marriage." I stayed sulky until the late afternoon. I knew he didn't like to go to sleep without reconciliation. He came to me, put his arms around me.

"I'm sorry. It was insensitive. I promise, I'll never go alone anymore. I want you to be happy with me." He kissed me tenderly on my cheek.

I grinned. "Remember, we are parrotswe are inseparable."

"Yes, my love."

And I added, "Otherwise we never argue."

He smiled. "Let's keep it that way." I liked these moments of reconciliation. After that our nights were happy.

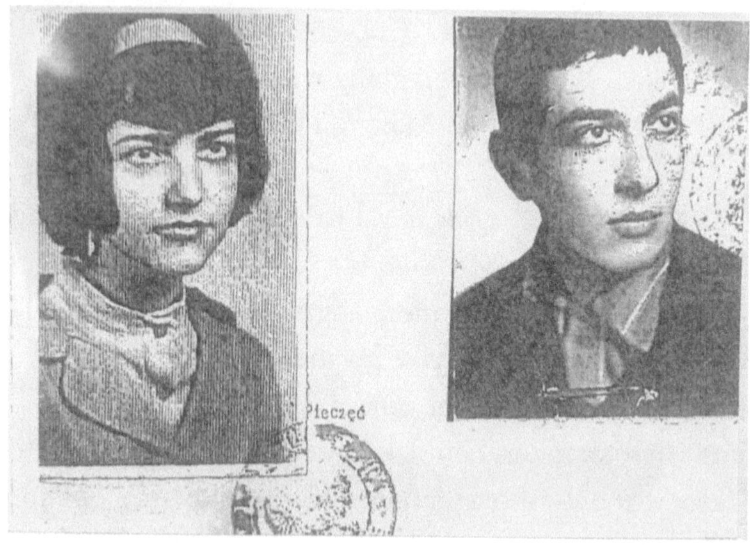

These photos came from our student's identity cards.

CHAPTER 23

TRIPS

One morning, Fitz woke up and was very silent. I was concerned. "What's happened?"

He answered, "I have my monthly headaches. It'll be for 3 days."

"Since when have you had these headaches?" I asked.

"Since my childhood. I took lots of aspirin. Sometimes it's so strong. Once I wanted to jump out of the window from the first floor."

"Where do you have this pain?"

"In the back of my head, above the neck."

Now I was worried. He had a stressful life because of his stepfather, a drunkard. I thought it over. What could I do to make him feel good? We kept drawing while we sat at a coffee shop. Fitz remarked, "Look at the hand of this woman. It's important to observe and draw it for a short time. This hand has its own expression. Every object has that. Like a rock on the road has its own life. It's like it has a soul. Observing and sharing enriches our minds. Touching the world by visual perception and feeling it."

Suddenly the idea came to my mind. "Would it be good to travel to other countries and see the museums?"

He had the smile of a dreamer. "Oh yes. But we don't have any money."

I replied, "We better start to put money aside. We have our Grants-in-Aid." We were raised in the communist system, isolated without the possibility of comparison with the rest of the world. Being an artist during that time made us the instant victims of the political censorshiplack of artistic freedomwhich created in us the feeling of imprisonment. However, in the Cracow museum we saw one beautiful example of Rembrandt and the famous Leonardo Da Vinci's "Cecilia Gallerani Portrait." It was a woman holding a weasel.

It was very difficult to obtain a passport during those years, and for an individual person it was almost impossible. The only way to travel abroad was to organize a group for students, ask for recommendations from the communist party, and get a group passport to travel. But it would only be to other communist countries. In order to do this, we had to become student communist party members. We had access to the party office and all the official stamps and printed forms.

Our first trip was to East Germany to see the

museum in Dresden. I remember a small painting of Rembrandt made when he was 19 years old. It was average art without the artist's personality yet. It gave us hope that later we too can become great.

The next trip we made was to Prague, Czechoslovakia. The architecture had an Italian flavor—a beautiful city, wonderful museum and legendary beer. The language had similarities to Polish, so we could understand. But the next country, Hungary, had a language so difficult for us, that we could only hear slur sounds without any distinction between the words. The museum in Budapest was great. Also we had famous goulash, very spicy and with a strong taste, meat with rich sauce cooked for a long time. We came back happy. Art was our window to the world.

One day I asked, "Would it be good to see Paris?"

Fitz replied, "Yes, but it would cost more money, and this summer I have military service."

I stayed positive on this idea. "We can stop buying canvas and put aside all our Grant-in-Aid, but I need to find some work."

He paused, "We have neighbors, two sisters from Russia they do decorative objects. Maybe they'll give you a job."

The old sisters were very nice. They gave me a set of small wooden cockerels (6"x5") and showed me how to decorate them. I had to use a small brush, making very fine, colorful lines, and that improved my hand. I stayed in bed and worked all day long. My sweet mother-in-law was bringing me food. One day the door opened suddenly, and I saw my husband standing there. Oh! What a moment of joy! Feelings of love were passing through meimmensity of love filled my world.

He came only for a few hours and had to leave. After he came back, he wrote cheerful recommendation letters to the passport office, signed, stamped and sent them along with our passport applications. Fitz received his passport first, and I didn't. I cried, because I knew that married couples rarely received permission to leave Poland together. After a few months my passport arrived. The year was 1967. We packed our suitcase with dry sausage, multivitamins and cardboard to paint. The door of a big world opened!

CHAPTER 24

HUNGER IN PARIS

Oh! ParisMecca for the arts! So we thought about it when we arrived in Paris. Two of our friends from Group A were already there, Mark and George. The first night was spent with twenty other people, mostly tourists, in a two-room apartment. We slept in the kitchen and everybody was passing by next to our bed. One girl passed by every morning without panties. I painted her later.

Some of the people were very hungry. Our sausage disappeared from the case, only our multivitamins were left. We had only $20 in our pockets. Mark got a job in a factory making plastic gloves. He had little salary and could not help us. He gave the advice to go to the farmers' market. "You'll find something, but be careful not to eat spoiled vegetables."

In Poland, we could easily live for two months on twenty dollars, but in Paris, only for several days.

Discovery of the new world was painful. In Poland, we never ate exotic fruits like oranges or bananas, and basic food like meat was very expensive. In Paris we saw mountains of everything, but we didn't have any money to take advantage of it. We didn't speak French yet. The language we heard on the streets was like a humming sound, continuous, without any distinction between the words. It took time to be able to hear the words at intervals and could start to learn.

It was hard to find something at the farmers market. Sometimes nothing was there. Every morning we went downstairs to see if we could find anything in the garbage can. Most of the time we could get French baguettes. It was the French custom to neatly pack day old bread and place it next to the garbage can or inside. Once, I heard something moving in the garbage can. We opened it and there were several baby rats. Now we knew who was stealing the bread from us. But they were so cute that I turned the garbage can down and let them go.

Fitz asked, "Do you feel good saving the rats?"

I grinned. "Maybe our neighbors saw us taking the bread from the garbage can, because they started leaving their baguettes outside of the door so we could take it." Baguettes dry up fast, and French people like them fresh. Searching for a job did not give much result because we didn't speak French yet, and had no legal status. We came as tourists on a 3-month visa.

French baguettes were very tasty, but having them

with only water wasn't good enough. Sometimes we couldn't find anything for several days. I felt humiliated, reduced to subhuman. I had hunger pangs. My stomach growled. Sometimes I felt dizzy and asked Fitz, "How do you feel?

He answered, "I'm ok. I'm a strong person. You'll see everything is going to be alright." I knew he didn't like to complain.

When I had stomach cramps, I imagined a leech, blood suckers, hundreds of them, stuck to my belly, sucking the life out of me. Sometimes I had nightmares. There were rats, big ones like an opossum, eating us alive.

I felt trapped in a cage, afraid of death, like a wild animal. In my sleepless nights, the fear of death came upon me. When I was worried, I would wake in the middle of the night. I realized that, involuntarily, I was sniffing myself to see if the process of decay had started.

He felt my anguish and kept whispering, "Don't worry, everything will be ok." He wrapped his loving arms around me. "Sleep well, my Sweetie."

CHAPTER 25

MILK, CHOCOLATE AND CIGARETTE BUTTS

I was tormented about our future, if we would get sick and never paint again. Should we come back to Poland? Should I ask him if he wants that? When I asked him about that, he said, "No, we should not come back to Poland, where we can predict our future without freedom or creation. Be more positive. It takes time. You never know what can happen here. We can try and dream and expect. We are young, strong and time will show that I am right to hope. You'll see."

His words were words of wisdom and consolation. I looked at him with admiration: "Ok let's take a risk and stay."

We were hugging and fondling each other soon. He said smiling, "I have good news. I discovered another French custom. We can steal some milk from the night delivery trucks leaving the bottles of milk under the doors. Each early morning we need to steal from different apartments. That will help us to survive."

One day a woman visited Marc. She was nice and gave us her telephone number to come and visit her. A few days later, we called her to see if she could lend 10 francs. She said she would. She did not know that we had no money for the subway tickets, so we had to walk to her home, maybe about 5 miles. She gave us 20 francs.

On the way back, we stopped before the store. In the window was a display of chocolate. We bought one and ate the whole chocolate instantly. A few minutes later I felt nausea, became sick and started to vomit. I became weak, and he held my arm and helped me to walk back to our room. But Fitz was stronger. He didn't have the same reaction. From that day, I didn't like chocolate for a long time. But the baguette with milk was so good! So good...

Another French custom was to give tips in the restrooms. There were small, flat plates for that before the entry. We started to steal the pennies. It was our survival. Our situation improved. We could buy coffee, two brushes to paint and even sometimes go to see a movie. One day we saw the movie based on the Knut Hamsun novel, "Hunger." There was one scene in it which we identified with, terribly. It was a fight between a man and a big dog over a bone. Both the animal and human were on fours, each pulling at the end of the bone toward himself. The man and the dog had spasmodic desperation for the life saving bone, to live at any price.

Suddenly we understood that a piece of art must bear the truth or otherwise it is impossible to identify with it and have any feelings about it. The truth, even painful, must be expressed, otherwise we would never understand the world we live in.

A few days later we were walking the street, where there were waterspouts on both sides. Suddenly I stopped. "I saw a sandwich in the shallow water. Oh, Fitz, look! It's big."

I started to bend toward it to grab it, when I heard his voice. "You're not going to go that low?" I felt ashamed. I didn't take the sandwich. I realized that it was not about the movie we saw, but in real life we are not the animals, because we have dignity.

But some time later, I saw my husband suffering. He had a terrible craving for cigarettes. He asked me to go to the street and find some cigarette butts. I felt his desperation. I couldn't say no. And he was a charming beggar. I went to the street and gathered a bunch of cigarette butts. When I came back, I smiled. "I just lost my dignity for you."

I saw his smirk. "It's different. You did it out of love for me. You sacrificed your dignity for me, and in my eyes, you became more beautiful than ever, because you had compassion for me. It was very human." He held me close, affectionately. Our kisses were the consolation for our bad situation.

CHAPTER 26

ODD JOBS, ODD LIFE

We needed to find a job, any job. The only way to become legal was to become a student.

Fitz decided to pass the entry exam at school of decorative arts in Paris, and he was admitted as the foreign student. In order to fulfill all requirements, he had to obtain official recommendation from the Polish Embassy in Paris. During that time in 1967, the Six Day War started, and the Communists became Anti-Zionist, many remained left Poland. Fitz didn't obtain a recommendation.

In about the same time, we got a letter from our last diploma year due to the new law forbidding the students to go abroad. After this, we decided to apply for political asylum. We felt expelled from Poland for good.

Fitz's first job was washing cadavers on which

autopsies were already made. Those dead bodies had to be cleaned so that the students of medicine could use them for their studies. Dozens and sometimes more than a hundred bodies of unknown people had to be washed every night. It wasn't easy for Fitz, but it was soon discovered that this kind of job was reserved for French citizens-it was relatively well paid. Fitz was fired.

I could find a job as a housekeeper. When the woman heard about my education, she said that I am overqualified, and she's too embarrassed to let me do her bed, so I had to leave.

I didn't say anything, just left with my head down. The second job was to sew gloves. When the time came to get paid, I got half of what I was supposed to get. The man said that he forgot to tell me that he pays for a pair, not for each glove. I got very little money. It was hard to make a living.

My next job was to watch two children, cook and clean the house. I had to work from 7am to 11pm.

The first month, I didn't get paid. When I was not paid for the second month, I understood that I needed to leave. I couldn't understand what kind of excuses people can find for their conscience, but when they are desperate or just see the opportunity to make money, they probably will find someway to justify their action.

I don't know what they saw in the mirror. Or they just thought that's what being smart was.

One day, the letter came from Poland with bad news. His mother died-from a heart attack.

He became very silent. The next day, he said, "I need to visit a cemetery."

When there, he stood without a word for a long while. My instinct told me that I should not say anything. What could we say that would be adequate with the immensity of existence? We were too young. Maybe we'll understand the meaning of all and our place in the world later…

In silence, I took his hand and he squeezed mine with affection. He knew I was with him and for him.

CHAPTER 27

JOBS AND ART

We were good to each other. We never argued angrily. We were attentive, sensitive and cared about each other. We learned about our differences and similarities. Sometimes, we were able to reach each other's minds. I started the sentence and he finished it, and vice versa.

But in art, at that time, we were very different. He wanted to express in symbols, searching for meaning. I was more light, influenced by Ukrainian fold ornaments. But we talked a lot. I wondered, "Will we ever be more similar in art, closer, like we are becoming in life?"

During this time, we painted, sometimes every day. We had our first exhibition with Group "A" in the Polish Center at Sorbonne University. It was April 1968. There were visitors at the opening, the people we didn't know, but nobody sold anything.

In 1969, we participated in "Salon des Artists Fran-
cois" and Zbigniew won an award there.

The Salon D'Automne (Fall Salon) was a very important event in artistic life in France. In the early seventies,
one of Fitz's paintings was accepted for the exhibition. It
was a large scale painting which Fitz, with his friend
Mark, transported, walking through all Paris from near
Montmartre where we lived, to Grand Palais, struggling
with the wind.

Canvas in the wind is like an umbrella, you can fly
with it and be smashed up at the end.

They arrived exhausted to the exhibition place and
learned that they missed the opening which took place
one day earlier, and there was no room for Fitz's painting, especially this big. Fitz and Mark took back the
painting, again walking several miles in the wind to our
apartment.

The next morning, Fitz woke me up and with difficulty said to me, "I can't move. I have a paralyzing pain
in my upper back."

I called the doctor to come immediately, but his
answer was, "He must come to me."

We understood this later as the doctor explained
what the problem was. It was neuralgia, provoked by
stress. The only way to ease the pain was to overcome it
by moving, exercising. He gave him some painkillers
and Valium and added, "You're gonna be better, when
you gonna have a success."

This sickness was coming back often, every time

provoked by stress, and all our big stresses came from problems concerning art, and the impossibility to do art full time.

The Parisian tradition for starving artists was working in legendary Montmartre, at the Place du Tertre, painting Paris landscapes or doing portraits for tourists. From an exterior point of view, it was a very picturesque place, but from inside it was a band of hungry artists from all over the world. Every square yard was jealously protected, and it took some real diplomacy and time to become one of them. Sometimes there were fights. The problem was also with French police who chased the artists who were aggressively asking the tourists to buy something or to pose for a portrait.

The prostitutes were arrested for exactly the same reason-solicitation. My husband didn't want me to work there. He was arrested once for soliciting to pose for a portrait by an undercover policeman. I wanted to bring him something to eat and to visit him in the police station. I could not believe my eyes. I saw the mixture of drunk prostitutes and Fitz with some other artists in the same cell. In Fitz's feelings, doing the idealized portraits of the tourists was really the same thing as prostitution.

After some time, he got terrible headaches as soon as he arrived at Montmartre, so I understood it was the time for him to finish this job.

Art for him was a responsibility, the question of

conscience. If you do something against yourself, it may kill you, slowly…

I traveled in my imagination to the empty cosmos asking, "Is there anybody there?"

I needed silence to hear a tiny whisper, "I'm here." I wasn't sure if it was real or if it was a voice of my desire. I guess I had to go through life without certitude, giving questions, seeking… but I'm a painter. My brush should bring answers, later in life, and Fitz was looking far into the horizon…hoping…dreaming…he had a very positive character, full of hope…

CHAPTER 28

MORE ODD JOBS AND FIRST GALLERIES VISITS

One day, the opportunity came for change when I heard some textile designer was looking for designers. I said, "I have to try that."

Fitz asked, "But you never did it before?"

I replied, "I have a good hand and the eyes. I'll look at how others are doing it."

And it happened as I pictured. I observed the designer next to me and quickly learned. But this job was only for one of us. I already had a good hand, sharp, clean and smooth lines were good for print. My boss discovered that if I had a good eye, I could do miniatures. He got an idea for me to do dotted designs, so everything was made from dots. I didn't need a magnifier. This idea worked well, so I had to do this all the time, all day long. After one month or two, I developed light sensitivity. I had to work with dark glasses. I couldn't work any longer. But I learned enough, so we could do freelance work and sell ourselves to the textile companies.

Finally, after a while, I got better and could do textile designs again.

We were avoiding taking a full time job. It would not leave time to paint. But freelance work had a lot of ups and downs-sometimes we could sell well or nothing at all. Finally, we decided to show our works in some of the Paris galleries. During one visit, the owner of the gallery paused and showed us the small corner on the upper right of the painting. "If you paint like this, I'll take it."

It didn't make sense to us. It would give abstract splashes with colors from Impressionism. We would be trapped in the corner of stagnation without chance of any progress. We were too young to have any defined style. We were not formed yet. We needed time to learn.

During this time (early 70s), Parish lost its title of being the art capital of the world.

New York became the new Mecca for art.

We looked at each other and said almost at the same time, "Now, New York." But we didn't have enough money.

Fitz, with his positive attitude said, "Don't worry, sometimes we are selling well. With a first good sale of the designs, let's take a vacation to check it out, a new Mecca."

I was so happy. "Good!" I flung myself into his arms. "I could not do without you."

He replied, "And vice versa."

We already started to build life baggage together. Problems made us closer to each other. Tender, long kisses, felt closeness and friendship went deeper. We dreamed, "Maybe in New York, somebody will notice us and give us a chance to develop like in Renaissance times?" We sighed. We were at our first exhibit in Paris, 1968.

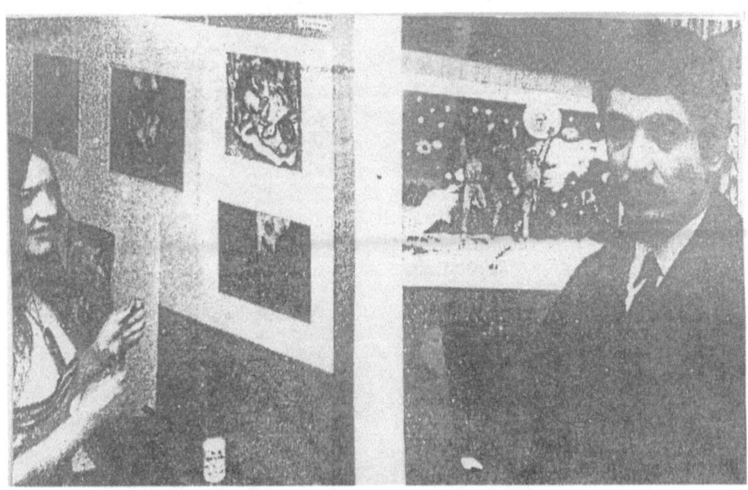

CHAPTER 29

TIME FOR CHANGE

We were ready to visit New York City. It was summertime in 1973. We took an airplane and arrived in the late evening. It was already dark when the plane stopped and the door opened. Suddenly, the head came so strong that I said, "Uh-oh!" and Fitz with his calm voice said, "Something is wrong. Something is broken." We looked around, everybody was quiet, going slowly toward the exit, so we followed them. To our surprise, outside was the same hot-that was the New York weather.

We took a taxi to go to the downtown hotel at Times Square. We saw skyscrapers standing tall and rhythmical, brightly illuminated. It was like stars fallen down to decorate Christmas trees. Somebody said, "This city never sleeps." It was very crowded.

Before entry of the hotel, several prostitutes tried to

stop my husband, offering themselves. In our room, I smiled. "They noticed a handsome man like you."

He grinned. "Am I?" He made a sign, "Come here."

I came to him, and put my head on his chest. "I'm tired."

He agreed. "You're right, let's go to bed. Tomorrow is going to be full of excitement." He caressed my cheek tenderly and I kissed him affectionately.

We woke up early and needed a coffee, so we went outside. It was packed with people from all over the world. Buildings covered with gigantic neon advertisements and vendors everywhere.

We wanted to see more of the city, so we took a walk from Broadway to the south. It was hot and humid. When we were crossing the streets, the heat from the cars blew like a heating furnace. But the streets were wide, so we didn't hear the passing cars.

The buildings were spectacular. Skyscrapers created grand canyons in elegant colors, brown and black, geometry of earthy monochromes or glass walled buildings with a reflection of clouds going through. We couldn't stop saying, "wow!" We were marveled. It's a fantasyland, what an imagination! It was a mix of historical towers with Gothic and Art Deco with gold pyramids and decorative treatment with use of steel for structure and sometimes we saw a Greek facade. We thought it must be a church, but the sign said "Bank."

Towers in the cloud could go 70 stories high. We went very down south, and we stopped next to the New

York Stock Exchange with a huge Greek Revival building eight-stories with 52-feet high Corinthian columns. It's the world's largest stock exchange where fortunes are made or broken.

The streets with tall buildings gave the impression of being narrow where sharp light was falling down and changing into waterfall, likely because of the high humidity.

People were like lizards, half naked or well dressed or eccentric-just beautiful. I thought, "one day, I'm gonna paint that."

And I heard Fitz sigh. "I could paint all that."

CHAPTER 30

"MORE TO SEE"

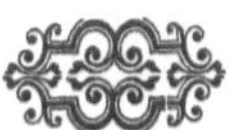

On the way back, from a distance, we saw the Empire State building, a 102-story Art Deco skyscraper, with a very colorful upper level. He said, "Let's go there."

I smiled and asked, "Are you gonna hang me over the city like you did over the river in Poland?"

He chuckled. "That was more than 10 years ago, and you have a vivid imagination. You know what I am gonna do?"

"What?"

"When we get high enough, I am gonna kiss you," and he brushed his hand against my cheek.

I paused, "But we need to see the museums."

"Let's go tomorrow to the Guggenheim museum. But before that, are you hungry?"

I nodded. There was a fast food place near the hotel, "Nathan's." It was cheap. We came back to Times

Square. It was crowded as usual, with all kinds of people. Friendly migrants, international visitors, vendors vying for attention, all kinds of people. They were very picturesque. America is made up of many different people. Walking was exhausting but exciting. We marveled and couldn't stop saying "Wow!" "Wow!" "Wow!"

It was wonderful, unique, full of energy, very stimulating for creation. We wanted to paint all this. We went to Nathan's. Food was tasty with a lot of everything.

We had a ham sandwich, very thick with meat. "Let's take this to the hotel. Tomorrow we'll take meatballs with macaroni and cheese." I felt so romantic, that I clung to him almost unconsciously.

He posed his hand on mine. "Are you happy?"

I looked deeply into his eyes and whispered, "yes." I melted. He was kissing my hand looking at me intensely, hypnotically. I wanted this instant to last forever. I asked, "Why do you love me after all these years?"

He answered, "When physical beauty is combined with wisdom and innocence, nothing can beat it. Nothing is more attractive than that."

I melted again. The chemistry between us was growing and our friendship was deeper and deeper. There were so many similarities between us.

We woke up early in the morning and went to the Guggenheim museum. The building was built by Frank Lloyd Wright for modern and contemporary art. The building was massive, white barrel, thick set and cold. But inside was spectacular with an open center,with walls of spiral design. We saw W. Kandinsky, Klee, Chagall, Mondrian, Picasso, Manet and the best was Van Gogh.

Temporary shows were less attractive to us. Art was easy, cold and impersonal.

Next, we went to MOMA, the Museum of Modern Art, the largest collection of paintings and sculpture, from the 19th century to the present. The best master-pieces were Van Gogh's "Starry Night", Picasso's "Les Demoiselles D'Avignon", Dali's "Persistence of Memory, and others. We also went to the Metropolitan Museum of Art-the biggest of all.

It is called an encyclopedia of the arts with two million square feet of exhibition space, which traces the history of art from 5,000 years, ancient, medieval art, the Egyptian, Greek and Roman or European works from Renaissance to paintings of Titian, El Greco, Rembrandt, also Ingres and Van Gogh.

Our cheeks were hot, and we were exhausted. It was a very emotional experience.

We got hungry, went to Nathan's, and took maca-roni, meatballs and cheese. We slept well that night. We woke up early and realized how time was passing fast. Time came to come back to Europe. New York made a great impact on us.

It was a wonder, unique, full of energy, very stimu-lating for creation. We both knew we had to come back, but how? It would take the money we didn't have.

But Fitz would never give up. "Don't worry, I'll think of something. You'll see, everything will be okay." I loved his optimism, it gave me comfort. I clung to him to feel security and hope.

We came back to Paris, dreaming about New York. But how to come back without money?

It was a time of problems for the textile industry in France. The work became scarce. We started to struggle to pay the bills. Going to America was not easy. It was a time of economic crisis, and it was almost impossible to obtain a Visa. I was worried and had many sleepless nights. I saw my husband worry too, thinking about the solution, and he kept telling me not to worry, but stay positive. But I was in such despair that I woke up one morning with terrible sickness. My stomach was seized by cramps. I had a headache, and I was vomiting every ten to fifteen minutes. Since I didn't eat anything, vomiting was dry, until I started to see the blood.

My husband went to the pharmacy and was told that

I have a stomach spasm. Under the strong stress, food stays in the stomach, doesn't go any farther and it results in poisoning.

The medication, some kind of sedative, didn't help since I couldn't absorb anything, not even the water. The pharmacist advised me to buy Coca-Cola. I forced myself to swallow sip by sip and after several hours, for some reason, it seemed to help. Finally, exhaustion brought relaxation, and it stopped. Since then, each time of prolonged stress, the spasm comes back, but not for so many days like the first time.

One day, Fitz said, "I have an idea."

"What's the idea?" I asked.

He replied, "Since it's so hard to get to the USA, let's go to Canada. If we go to Montreal, it's very close to New York. Canada is accepting immigrants. They even help to find a job."

Looking down, I was skeptical. "Even going there, we need money."

He never gave up. "I'll think of something."

One day, he said, "I heard that the Jewish are helpful, so let's try to ask them for help."

We went to the French-Jewish organization "Societe Israelite de Demarrage Economic" - Israel Company of Economic Start. They lent us money to travel, and we applied for Canadian immigration Visas. We were accepted. We packed our books and some paintings and were ready to go. It was a beautiful springtime in 1974. With new life, new hope will come.

CHAPTER 32

FROM PARIS TO MONTREAL

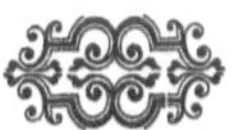

Early April, 1974, we left Paris and went to Montreal, Canada. April in Canada was cold and the snow was grey, dirty, not white. The Canadian official came to the airport to meet us. One of the first questions was, "Do you have any money?

I answered, "Yes, we have $1,000."

So she found the apartment for which we had to pay. We didn't worry because we were promised to get a job at the publishing house as illustrators. But at the Canadian Embassy in Paris, they forgot to tell us that the publisher was German, and we needed to speak the German language. So, in Montreal, they found us a job in a factory of T-shirts as designers, but it was for only one person, for $500/month. I didn't like to stay home alone, so I went to work for free with my husband.

We discovered a cheap Kentucky Fried Chicken, which we liked very much, without knowing that it was considered junk food. Soon, it became clear that it's too hard to make a living. So, we started to think about New York.

We did a group of textile designs, a beautiful flower with our good hands. For the rest of the money (which was left from Paris), we bought a used car, almost junk, and left for New York. There were no problems to pass the border, nobody was checking. We were a little worried if we had enough dollars to pay for the hotel.

I said, "We have to go to any textile company as fast as possible."

He said, "Yes, we'll go first thing in the morning." I was a little nervous, but also happy to see New York again. He was positive. "Don't worry. Everything will be okay." We couldn't sleep. He wrapped his hands around me. I felt a tiny shudder rippling through him. It also gave me a kind of pleasure. After all the years, the chemistry between us got stronger and stronger.

I was looking at his sculptured, sensual lips. He was not only good looking, he was breathtaking. I cuddled to him to feel security. Together we could face the world with great hope and expectations. I felt warmth and went to sleep.

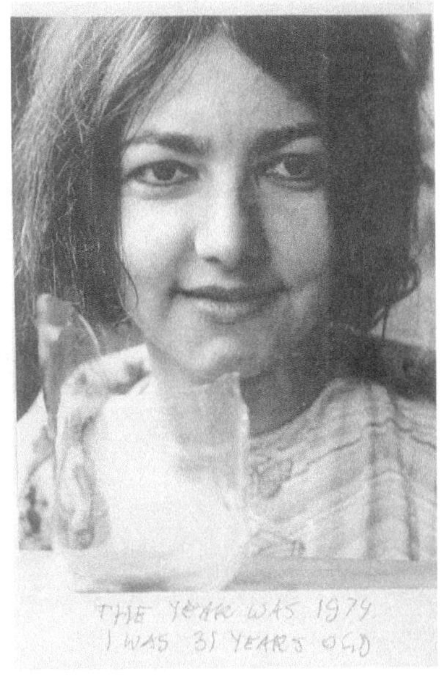

THE YEAR WAS 1979.
I WAS 31 YEARS OLD

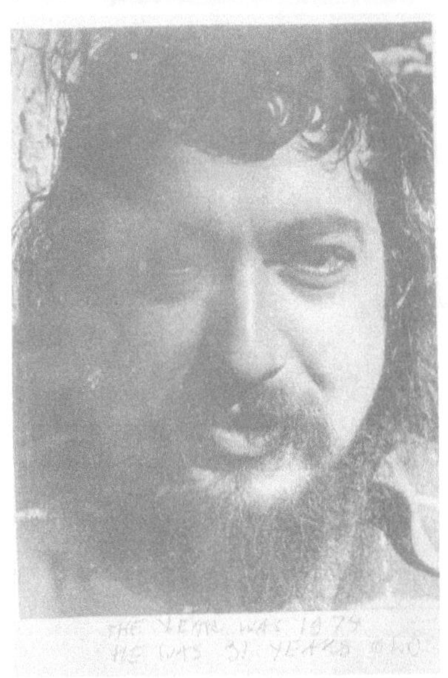

THE YEAR WAS 1979.
HE WAS 31 YEARS OLD

CHAPTER 33

STARTING IN NEW YORK

We woke up early with anxiety. Our concern was if we'd sell anything. We took our portfolio and went to Downtown. Broadway was the center for many companies. We stopped in the middle of skyscrapers. We chose the tallest one at 1359, went inside, and noticed Concord fabrics. We looked at each other, no need for words, we could read each other's minds. We took the elevator. There was no Floor 13, that would bring bad luck. We showed our designs. The first company we presented our work to reacted with surprise and joy. "We have been looking for you for some time now. We saw your work in a German fashion magazine, and we would like to have you both as our designers."

We said, "We need to go back to Canada and pack."

They replied, "There's no need for you to go back

there. Ask somebody to send your things. We'll pay for the shipping."

So, we started to work for them right away. Year 1974 was a difficult time to obtain a Visa. They paid the lawyer $2,000. The reason for us to stay in the USA was that we were specialists in miniature work. We could not be replaced.

Our first apartment was in the suburb, Queens. It was one room in the basement. We took the noisy subway. When we opened the door coming from work, the room was full of cockroaches. When we sprayed, they went to the ceiling and started to fall down our bed. That was a nightmare. But that didn't stop us from loving America. Later, Fitz was going to make a drawing, *Cockroaches in New York*, a very good composition.

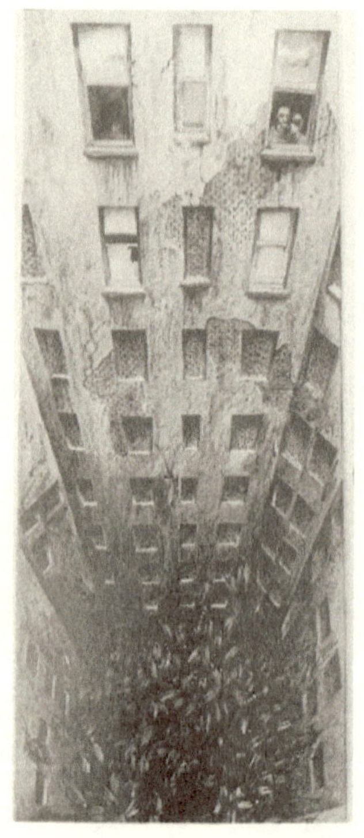

After a while, we rented a studio at West 64th Street, facing the Lincoln Center Metropolitan Opera House. Our apartment was on the 26th floor with breathtaking views of the city.

CHAPTER 34

"OVERTIME" 1975

Our boss, Mrs. Beth Dessler, was very good in her domain. She knew what sells well and how to make you work at your maximum. When demand for our designs began to grow, we had to spend all our time doing them. When everybody left the job at 5 o'clock, we had to stay until 7 o'clock every day which made for us 10 hours of work a day. She was coming very often to the studio, usually to ask to change something. When you have to change one element of a flower, you have to change the whole design.

Sometimes the design was almost done when she wanted us to do it again. It was irritating because it looked like she was playing with us. Especially, she liked to bully my husband since he was gentle and never said anything. But I was giving her my angry look.

One day, she came and said, "I need to talk with you." She continued, "You need to get serious about this job. I need you to work on weekends."

When I asked, "Why do we need to work so much?"

She replied, "Remember, we paid your lawyer. You have to pay back."

Every Monday morning, we had to bring her the work we did during the weekend. Each time she asked, "That's all you did?" It didn't matter how hard we worked, the question was always the same, "That's all you did?"

Since we had stability, we started to think about buying a house somewhere in a suburb of New York. I started to train myself not to go to the store and buy any new dress. We also started to do more designs at home, usually at night, to sell later at another company. We needed the money for a downpayment. We became so tired that after work, we didn't look up at New York buildings to see the rainbow reflecting in the windows. But we felt positive to look for a house.

Finally, we bought one, 25 minutes from New York. It was in north Mount Vernon, very close to Westchester, an exclusive place with lots of big houses. The house was a beautiful Tudor style with a small yard, but facing a big garden of the neighbor. The house was big, three bedrooms. That was a happy moment.

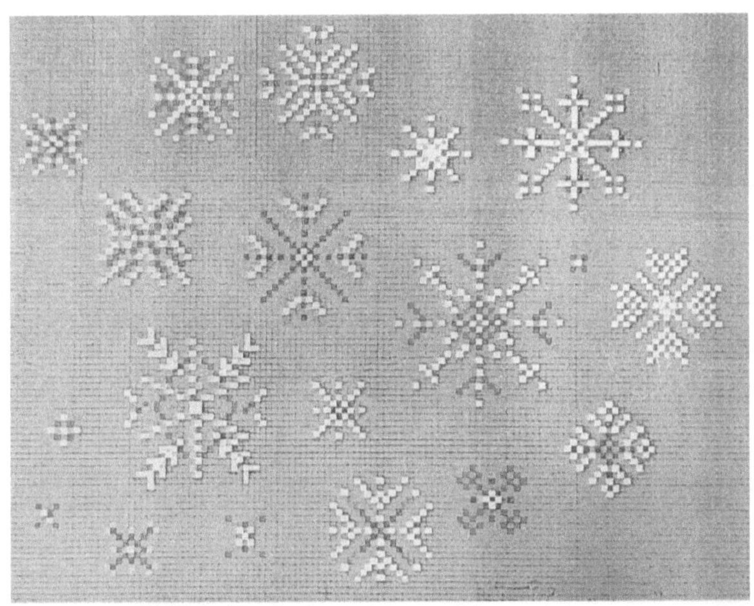

Zbigniew Fitz - Trial design for Textile 1974

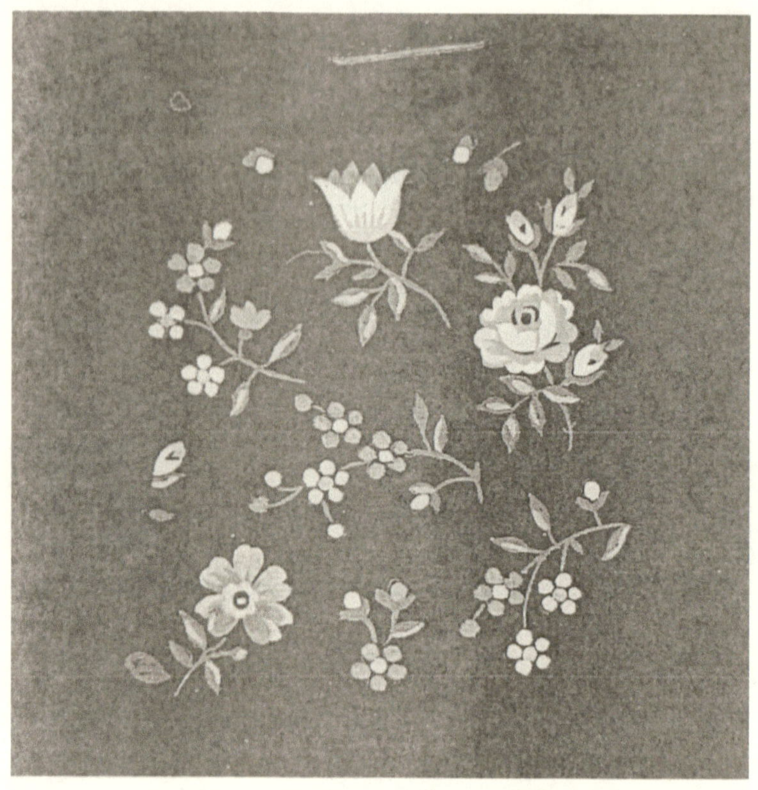

Emilia Fitz - Trial design for Textile 1974 Natural Size

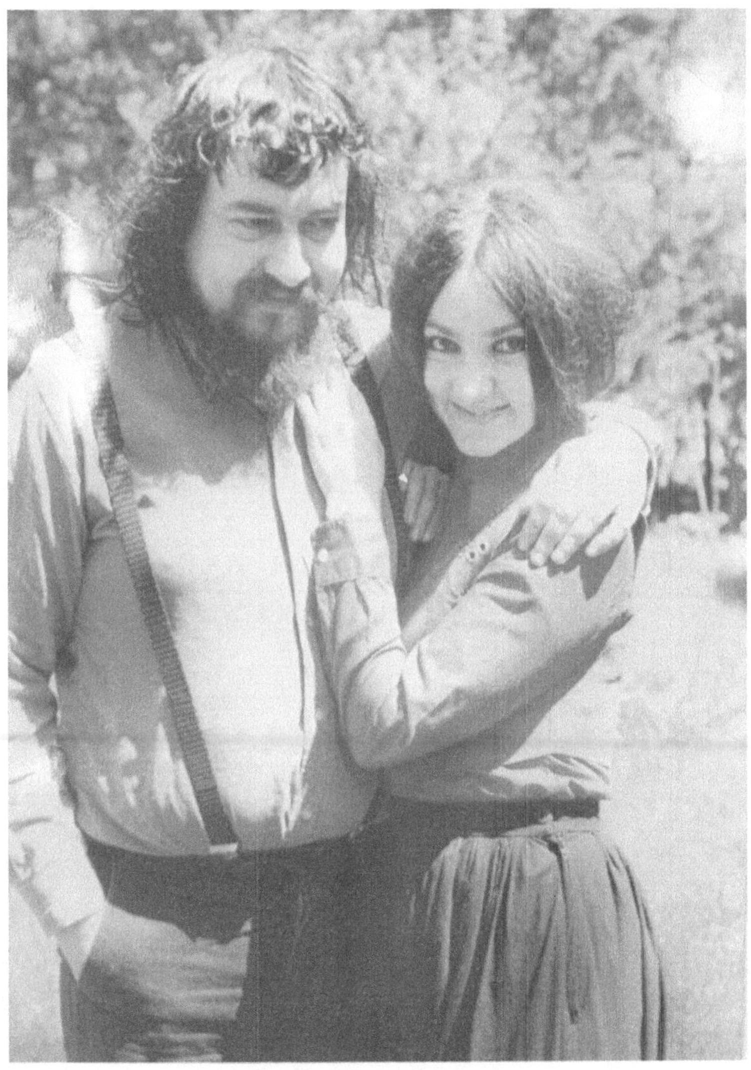

The time came to take vacation. They gave us one week. We took one more week and sent them our photo without giving the address.

CHAPTER 35

IF ONLY WE COULD KNOW OUR FUTURE.

It was Monday morning. As usual, we brought our homework, and as usual we heard, "That's all you did?"

My blood was boiling, but we didn't say anything. After a few hours, our boss called my husband to her office (our working room was just next to it.) Suddenly, I heard a loud noise, a slamming door. I whispered, "that's my Fitz." Fitz with his iron hand-he made our room shake.

The next moment, I saw him stand in the door, he was very pale. He made a sign with his hand. "Let's go. Take everything with you." I didn't say a word. I could see it was serious. We left the company. I didn't say anything. He was agitated, in a troubled state of mind. He broke with silence. "Do you trust me?"

I answered. "Yes, with every fiber of my being. Even

if we lose something, I will not regret it, and I'll go with you to the end of the world."

He wrapped his hand around my arm. "You are my one and only." His voice choked up with emotion.

I put my head on his chest, and he cuddled me close to him. We were walking the streets looking south at the tall buildings, majestic and indifferent. We came to our apartment, had dinner in silence and went to bed. I started to question, "What happened?"

He replied, "I got fired."

"Whaaat?"

"Yeesss."

"But… but.. You have a better salary than mine."

He answered, "She was playing the game. She said that I'm not pushing you enough to do more."

I paused, "You know that I would listen to you, but I also know you would never do that."

It was humid, sticky, muggy. When we passed the street, cars were standing in line and terrible heat was coming from them, like a fire from a kitchen stove.

I wanted to continue my questions when I heard, "Shhhhh."

He pulled me toward him and started to kiss gently, emotionally, the trust ignited desire… The world disappeared…

We woke up optimistic. The first question that came to me was, "Can artists become good without a gallery?"

He replied, "Yes, it's even betternot to be influenced.

Listen to your inside voice. Your instinct will tell you what is right in art. We need to paint every day. Just to be honest and don't think about money."

Second question I asked was, "Can an artist make money without a gallery?"

He replied, "Time will show. If we do great art, somebody should notice and give a chance to our potential, and will support us like in the Renaissance in Italy. Rich people were proud to discover the talent by themselves."

I added, "Whatever will come, we made a big decision." It was the year 1976.

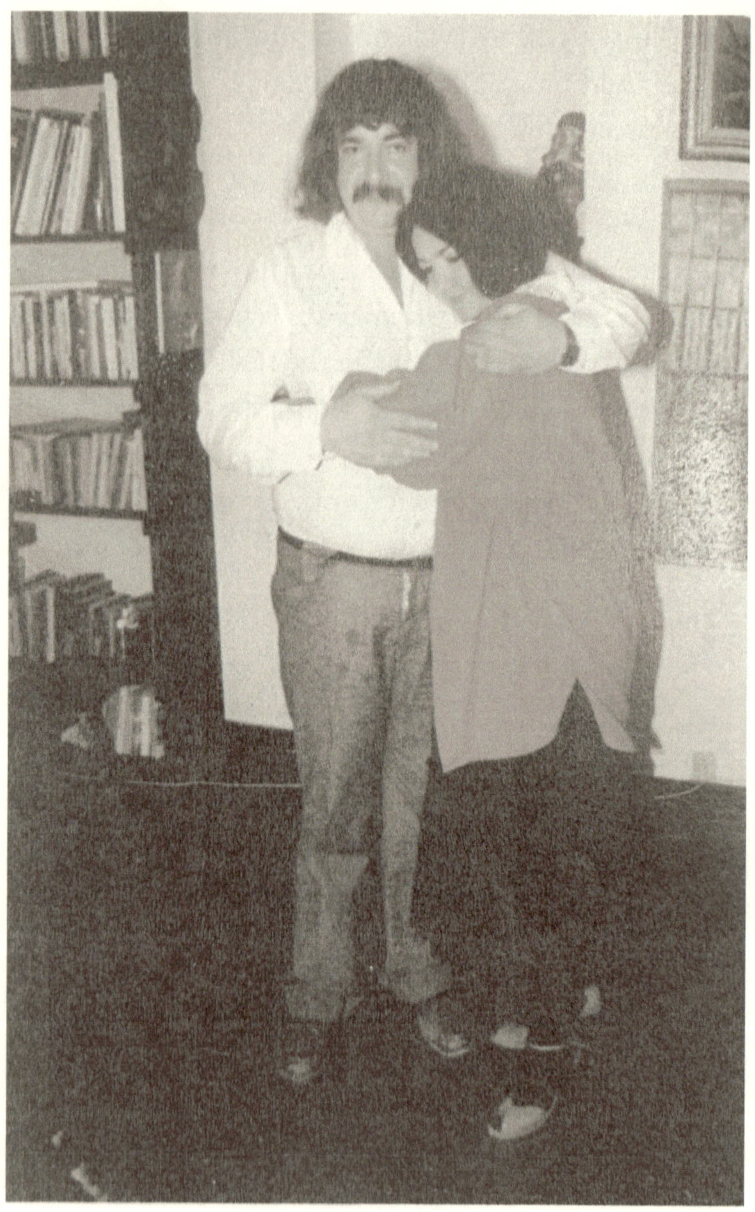
152   LOVE TO DEATH

CHAPTER 36

THE YEAR OF HOPE 1976-77

We already bought a house with a small yard. It was a Tudor, big enough to paint and do textile designs. Mortgage was not very high. It was a nice, sunny day. Fitz was smiling. "I got it out of my mind that we should take a one week vacation, and then start to paint."

I asked, "How are we going to make a living?"

"Don't worry," he said. "We are very successful in this company, so we should work as a freelance part time." It brought comfort to my mind.

We discovered garage sales where used stuff was very cheap. Fitz was looking for more jeans and denim shirts, and I liked dresses. We liked to go to the forest whenever I saw something pretty, I was digging and planting in our garden. Once I brought a nice plant with shiny leaves. Next day after planting, I started to be covered with pimples, itching terribly. The doctor told me it was poison ivy. That was a good lesson to not trust anything looking nice.

One day, we were just talking. His voice was mellow and pleasant. The telephone rang, abruptly. I heard him answer, "This is him." A woman's voice asked something, I could not hear what it was. Before he answered, he hesitated for a moment, "We are not coming back." The voice continued. He paused, "You were mean, nasty – goodbye."

"Was it our boss?" I asked.

"Yes, she said she was joking."

We were happy and optimistic, doing something we always wanted to – paint. She telephoned every day for two weeks. After a week, he had an idea and asked me if I wanted to paint it, whoever wants this more.

We painted in the same room. There was no jealousy, no competition between us. The only competition we had was with ourselves. Each next painting had to be better than the previous one. The colors he liked were green, gray and black. We were very different from each other. I was more naive. I sighed. "I wish, one day, we'll become more similar, closer, like in our life." We get to paint or draw every day. He had a good professor – he was trained "Not a day without a stroke."

I started to ask him to stop smoking. He said one day, "You are nagging me. I smoked since I was 12 years old, now it's too hard."

I replied, "I don't want to dispute, but it's no good for you – please, try."

"I'll try, one day."

I responded, "Don't make fun, it's serious."

He assured me, "I'll try, I'll try."

The time came to make an exhibition. We were invited to the group exhibit with two more artists from Poland. The year was 1977. It was in Washington D.C. at the Dimock Gallery, George Washington University. "Metaphorical Trends in Art." Small group of students came to the opening. Some of them liked wine served at the openings. Not one of us sold anything. We came back after several days. Nobody was there. The only visitor was a dog. My husband took a photo of him.

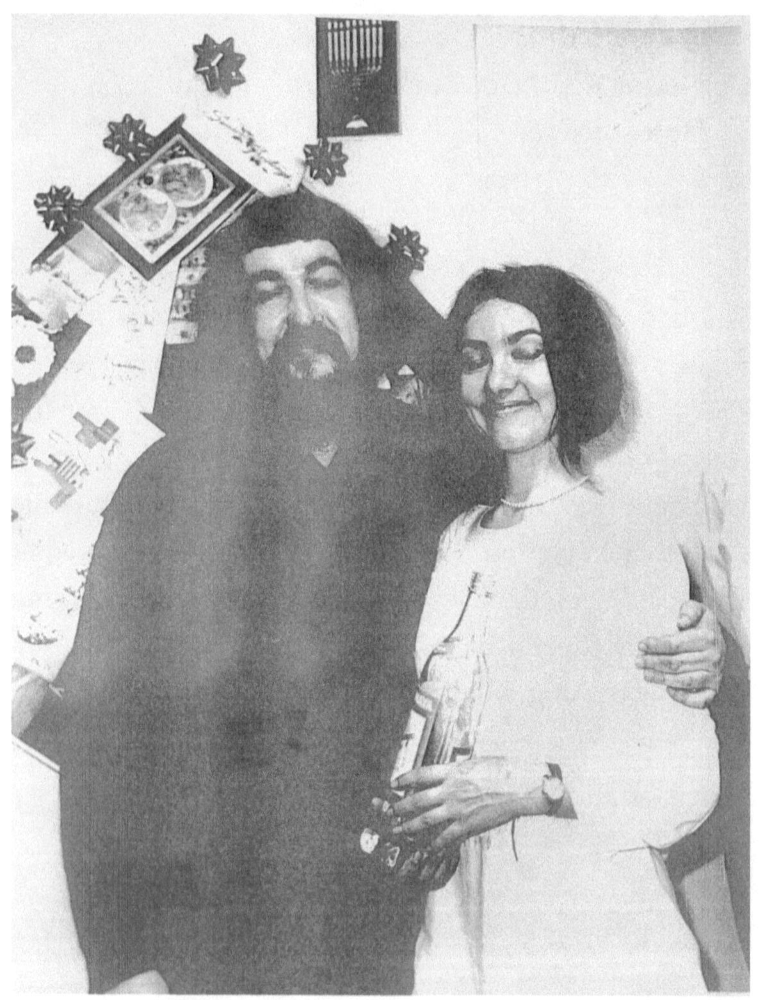

CHAPTER 37

FUTURE MADE BY OUR DECISIONS

One day, we started to have a desire to have a child. We stopped on the street each time we saw a child.

I had a little medical problem which made it very difficult to get pregnant. The only thing I needed was to go to the hospital for the surgery, which I did. The doctor said, "Now you can have children."

I went home happy. After the sleepless night, the panic came, and I woke up crying. With a life without stability, a child against art will always win. So we will never paint again. Fitz brushed his hand against my cheek and said, "Don't worry, we don't have to have children. We'll concentrate on art."

I melted inside and was grateful for understanding. I was smiling warmly. Finally, we realized that very little money was left. We had to face reality. Mortgage was not very high, but taxes for the house got bigger and bigger.

He made an appointment, took our portfolio and went to New York City. It was 30 minutes to downtown by car. He took me in his arms and placed a delicate, almost elusive, kiss on my forehead. I felt it was a tiny, subtle flicker of love. When he came back, I saw from the window his sad face. He opened the door – the only word was "Nothing."

I smiled. "There's always next time."

He grinned politely. I felt his gaze and I drowned in his deep, dark eyes. Many days followed like this. I stayed home to do more designs, but no result. He was surprised.

"I don't know what they are looking for, they never say anything." He said one day, "I'll think of something."

A few days later, he said with excitement, "This time it should work. We need to sell this beautiful house, move to the countryside and become self-sufficient."

I nodded. "And we'll have more time for art, but before we go any further, I'd like to make one more trip to the city."

He burst into laughter. "We are not going to be very far – about 1 to 2 hours from the city, but let's go to see one more time."

I just wanted to walk through the streets, to feel the crowd, to be close to everything. It was hot and humid. I looked around, and I saw beautiful, colorful people.

Most women wore high heels. When we walked toward the south, all of a sudden, I felt powerful, caring arms surrounding me, and I clung to him. Skyscrapers were standing straight up, rhythmically, in rows of geometric, splendid forms gleaming in sunshine with almost dark pastel colors. I also thought about Picasso and his cubist period.

The incredible height of the buildings made it look like the Grand Canyon. Fitz asked, "Where's it gonna be the end of the world – in the Grand Canyon or here, in New York City?" I smiled, trying to picture this image. I suddenly hear Fitz. "I'm hungry, aren't you?"

I nodded. "I like pizza, pepperoni with double cheese." We walked, smiling, looking for a pizzeria.

CHAPTER 38

HEAVEN

The year was 1980. We had a new home in the countryside, between Middletown and Port Jervis. It was two hours from New York City. It was so beautiful, and I was so moved, I couldn't talk. I was in the deep of the forest, three acres of land, with a small stream. The inside of the house was all wood, two bedrooms, smaller than the previous Tudor.

A big window showed a view for a future garden. When we were ready to go to bed, Fitz took two glasses and the bottle of red wine, Zinfandel. He opened it and said, "Let's celebrate our new life." One glass made me sleep fast.

We woke up happy, took a deep breath and went to walk to the forest. It was springtime – breathtaking. We had our first kiss in our new life, like a promise for a good future.

Rhododendrons were in full bloom, all white 3 to 5 feet high. They were everywhere. We had some money left from selling our previous house, so we quickly asked local people to cut the trees in front of the house, tilled the garden space, ordered a full truck of aged cow manure and put some fence against the deer. Everything grew fantastic, like zucchini reaching 18″ long and flowers, flowers, flowers… breathtaking. It was heavenly.

However, it was more work and harder than we expected. Fitz was sweating a lot.

Soon we had geese, rabbits, one goat, a big dog (Newfoundland) and a cat. Every morning, we all took a walk to the forest, but the rabbits didn't go with us. Some time in the middle of the summer, we saw more and more gypsymoths. It was hard to walk, because they were everywhere. Slowly our forest changed. The leaves were eaten and by the Fall time, all leaves disappeared.

Time came to prepare for the winter. We ordered a truck of wood for fire. We also brought a big furnace to the basement. We enjoyed some colorful leaves and waited.

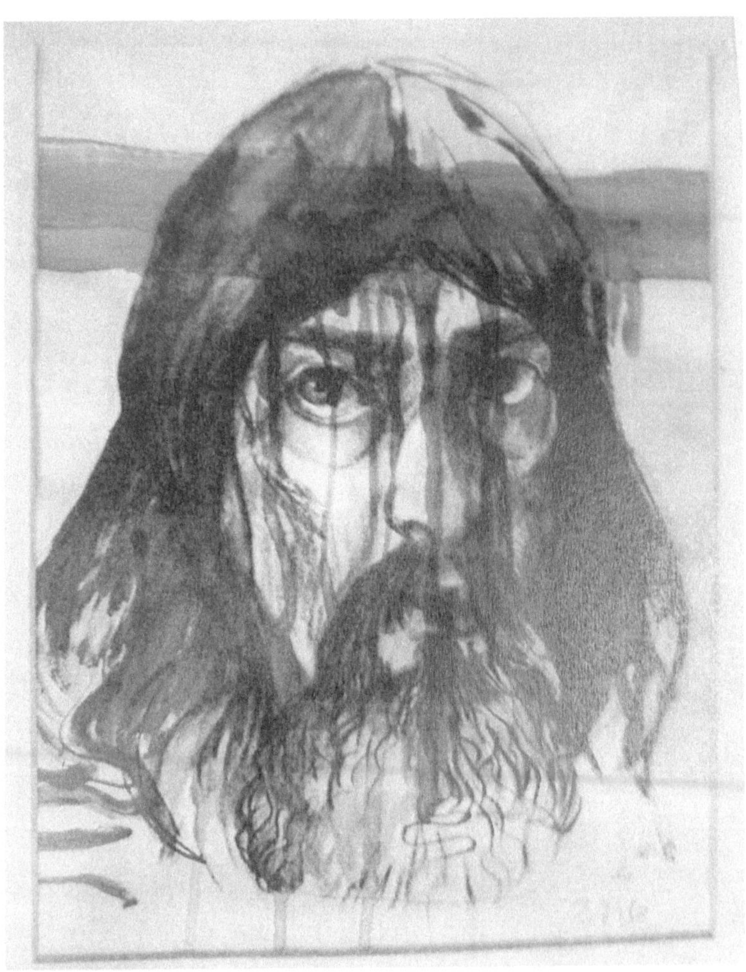

Zbigniew Fitz 1984 "Self" 13 ½" X 11" Crayon/Aquarel/Paper

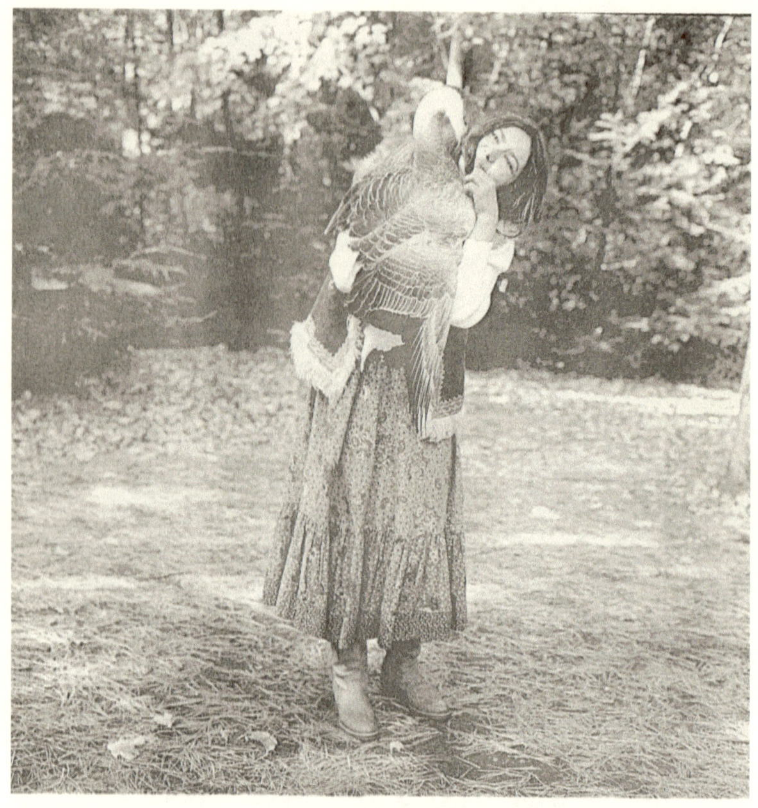

I loved all our animals, and none had a fear of us. Goose were free to go to the stream. When I called "Goosey, goosey, goosey," they all came running fast toward my voice.

CHAPTER 39

HELL

It was Fall, time to prepare meat for the winter. We had a gun, so Fitz killed them all little by little. We went to the basement to skin the rabbits first. I never did that before, and I had to overcome some nausea. Fitz was watching, so I had to be strong. When we prepared the rest and put it in the freezer. We had to wait for about 6 months. We could not eat them. They were our pets. Winter was coming fast. It started to get cold. We had to use the wood to heat the house. The big furnace took a lot of wood. We had to bring the wood inside the basement all day long. It was exhausting.

We were struggling for several seasons and almost out of cash. From time to time, we sold some designs, just to survive. For designs, each company had its own style without saying that in the open. No matter how many animals that you raise, it wasn't giving you the cash, and that's what you need to pay the bills. Even taxes were steadily going up. We had no more choice. We had to take a full-time job. It was two hours from New York City, so two ways it was a four-hour drive. When our boss learned that we travel four hours a day, he said, "You must be tired. You cannot be efficient enough. I have to fire you."

So, we stayed in the middle of nowhere without any money. It was cold, so Fitz got a toothache. After too many Tylenols, one day he fell down. It was a shock. I was kicking the colorful leaves, angry, without knowing why. It became clear that we have to change something, even if we did something wrong, we had to do something.

After visiting the doctor, he had high blood pressure. He added, "the wine will help with the stress." With hotdogs every day, he had a glass of wine. When I realized that he took two glasses, I started to drink one glass so that it would not be enough for him. I was concerned with his smoking. "You have to stop. With your health problems, it won't help - it will get worse."

"I'll try," he replied.

I got irritated. "No more try. You have to stop, that's an order."

"Yes, my darling."

I didn't see him smoking at home anymore. One day I didn't see him outside, so I went to look for him. He was hiding behind the storage – smoking.

I got angry. "If I see one more time, I'm not gonna talk to you."

He was a peace-loving person. He didn't like to see me angry. He did quit! I could relax.

One day, we didn't pay electricity, so there was no hot water. The taxes were too high – from $700 the first year, it went up to almost $5,000 in five years. We called our friends without being sure if they would be able to help us. These good people loaned us $4,000 – a big break in our misery. When we were driving to their house, I was looking at the sun and asked, "How come the sun is still shining?" and I asked in my silence, "God, if you exist, make them rich."

How to keep faith in anything? If we say, "No more hope," it would mean death of our inside. It seemed ugly, and we refused that. Hope must be somewhere… What about art? It's still there, in our hands and souls - that's hope. No more energy to paint, but the hope is still there – it's dormant.

We finally understood why we very rarely could sell anything. Because we had to fit. Each company had its own style that they never talked about, maybe because they were waiting for surprise - something similar to their need but somehow different. To most of them, we didn't fit. The only company we could fit was the one who invited us to the USA. We discussed that, and I called without knowing if they'll accept us. To our surprise, they were glad to hear from us. We started to work for them as a freelance even if they preferred us to work full-time for them.

When I saw my husband's health was deteriorating, I wanted to save him. One sleepless night brought me a new idea. We needed to change the climate. The best for it was to come back to Europe, to France, since we could speak French. The south of France was dry. But how to get money to buy a house there?

I just realized how much this company needed us. A crazy idea came to my mind. I told Fitz, "my idea is to ask them to borrow $20,000. For that, we could buy a small house."

Fitz said, "you need to have guts to ask them for that. How will you give this money back?"

I paused. "Why don't I ask them for royalty?"

Fitz burst into laughter. "I never heard that."

So, the next morning, I called them to see the boss. When I asked her for the royalty, she was surprised and said, "no designer ever got royalty."

I smiled, trying to cover my nervousness. "There's always a first time."

It took a few days to call us back. "Okay, we'll accept that. We are preparing the contract."

We got $20,000. "You'll pay back from the sale of your work, we'll deduct it," said the boss. For the south of France, I supposed we'll work for our company, since we didn't have any other source of income for a living.

Fitz called me that he found a nice, small house in the village, houses made from rocks, with a mountain view in the distance, wth 150 population (not including suburbs), mostly vacation houses.

Several days later, I got a call from our boss. She was angry. "You're not supposed to work for any competing company. So, keep working for them, you won't get any work from me." I had no chance to respond, she hung up.

How are we going to make a living in France? Before I could answer my question to myself, I got terrible chest pain. It was so strong, I couldn't move. I thought that I had a heart attack, and I'm home all alone, and I didn't work for anybody else at that moment.

I waited a minute and called my husband. I was in panic, talking quickly with difficulty breathing. "Come back home fast. I lost the job, and I'm sick." I waited another few minutes and slowly went to bed.

I was afraid to make any move.

Next day, I stayed in bed. When I heard my husband coming, I felt him covering me with a blanket, and I felt care. So, I was alive, it was not a heart attack. I didn't know that stress can give this kind of pain, but he was here, next to me, and I was loved!

It was a beautiful, late spring of 1985.

May 21, 1990

To: Emilia & Zbigniew Fitz
From: Martin Wolfson
Subject: Loan & Royalty Agreement

Enclosed is a calculation of the "Fitz" royalty for April, 1990. The $896.57 earned in April reduced the loan balance from $1653.07 to $756.50.

Regards,

lifschitz

CONCORD FABRICS INC. · 1359 Broadway, New York, N.Y. 10018 · (212) 760-0300

CHAPTER 41

ROBBERY

I woke up scared for our future. Fitz was sitting on the side of the bed with the sweetest, warm smile. He took my hand. "Before I'll bring you the coffee, I have to tell you something. You don't have to worry anymore. The house I chose is in the middle of a stone village. It's so rustic, tourists are coming from all over Europe. There's lots of galleries, so painters are selling. There's also beautiful mountains far away, all hillsides are covered with flowers: yellow, blue and white, you're gonna like it."

This vision made me smile, and the coffee was very tasty with cream and sugar. Smiling, I said, "I have to see it."

He smiled back. "We can go right away, before selling the house."

"We have debts. I don't know if anything will come from the sale."

He was very optimistic, as usual. "We'll see. It's a very nice property." I jumped from the bed and started to pack.

The next day, we took a trip to Europe, two-ways. We stopped in Nice, in our friend's apartment. To our village was a two-hour drive – we rented a car. It was real countryside. Passing through the forest, we reached our place. The village was on the top of a small mountain, like hanging from the sky. It was breathtaking. The house was small but just right for the two of us.

"Where's the gallery?" I asked. It was in the wine cellar. There were no steps. We had to jump two to five feet down. Temperature was perfect, but no light yet. We slept in our friend's apartment, and before that we went to the restaurant.

We had a good time. When we came to the car, to our horror, we were robbed. Me, stupid, I left all papers in there, including airplane ticket. They took everything, even big, dark cherries we bought for the road.

My husband always kept his papers with him.

So, he had to come back to the USA alone. I had to stay in our friend's apartment. His wife was very happy, she could have somebody to talk to. Her husband was almost never home. My first night was a nightmare. I was screaming in my dream.

GAP

I felt a huge gap between me and my husband. This gap was the Atlantic Ocean. I was on the brink of ruin. I was married for 22 years, and I was never separated from him. It was the year 1985, and I was 43 years old. Our friend, Mark W. said, "If you keep crying like this all the time, I'll wait for the rain and I'll put you on the street."

His wife, Chick, 20 years younger than him, was laughing. "He's not gonna do that."

He said, "You just watch me." Instead of crying, I took a bottle of vodka and started to drink, especially before I went to sleep. Mark's wife, Chick, was talking a lot. To take a rest, I went to the farmer's market. I saw an impressive dandelion – it was cultivated for a very delicious salad. Its leaves were 10" to 12" long.

I also went to the nearby park and Mark said, "You

cannot go alone. It's dangerous." I was reading the history of America to apply for citizenship.

I asked Mark to drive me to the American Consulate. It was to Marseilles, two hours drive from Nice. I asked them to give me the passports, but they said, "Without any papers, we don't know who you are." I went there once a week – each time it was the same answer. My husband was calling Washington D.C. every day, and he got the same answer.

When the fourth week was coming, I decided to stay there in the Consulate, no matter what. I told them that I'm not leaving. They can do anything they want with me.

So the lady called to Washington and somebody on the phone asked me, "When you say you lived in New York City, where did you pay your taxes?"

I said, "In Albany." My answer was perfect. It was a tricky question because New York City, even gib, is not a capital, but Albany is. They gave me my new passport instantly. Holding the passport, I burst into tears. I couldn't hold back crying. Mark suggested I drink some coffee. He also ordered vodka. I let him drink. I didn't. I quickly packed and bought an airplane ticket. I had to take the bus to Paris. When I got on the airplane, my hands were sweating from the emotion.

When I arrived in New York, I can't describe what I felt. To see my love again, it was a dream come true.

I asked him, "How did you pass the days?"

He whispered, "I was sitting on the sofa, without

doing anything. I had depression, so calling to Washington was my daily occupation." We were both moved deeply, staring at each other for a long while. We sold our house quickly. We paid debts, and we had $10,000 left for living and renovate the wine cellar to do the gallery.

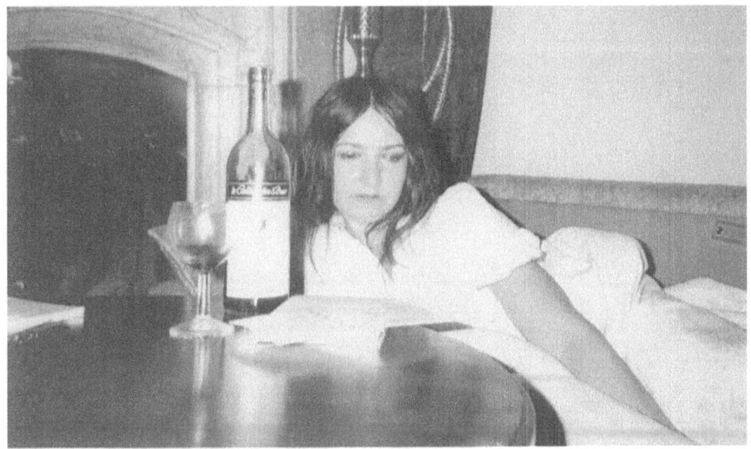

CHAPTER 43

NEW PLACE, NEW LIFE

Before going to France, we did our citizenship. I felt ashamed because I didn't answer the tricky question "How many stars does the American flag have?" and the man answered for me, "50, because we have 50 states."

We came to France with $10,000 left from the sale of the house.

The cost of living in France was more expensive, and we needed it for the gallery renovation.

After we were in our home, we took a walk through hilly terrain – it was springtime – all covered with flowers: yellow, shrubs, pink wild roses and spots with mallows, in all colors, five feet high. It was heavenly.

One day, looking up, I asked, "What's behind the sky?"

Fitz paused, "The music."

I liked his answer so much that I said, "Why don't you paint that?"

And he did. The sky was abstract, colorful with violin emerging from colors, under the sky were mountains and the Karajan conducting the universe. That painting was so beautiful, it talked to everybody who was watching.

We didn't have much time before we would spend money. First, we bought cement blocks to build the stairs to the gallery. Next, we had to have a good light and paint all the room pure white, the best for paintings.

And then the time came to paint. We noticed that all the paintings were small, that tourists could take it with them. Also, it had to not be expensive. The artist who sold the most was the one who painted bunches of chickens, very realistic, giving the illusion they were alive. It was small, 20" x 15". When we painted something, it had to be very detailed and worked for "ever". The best were rich in objects. It took a long time to do it, and it almost didn't pay off. If painting took two months, the tourist would not pay more than for one month of living.

It didn't take very long to realize that this kind of painting took all of our creative energy. That was another trap. The one thing we knew was that we cannot face the world before being ready to offer something new and high quality. We kept searching, mastered our skills, but nothing could satisfy us about our art.

With small sizes (20″ x 15″), we couldn't breathe - to do it in ground style, we needed bigger space in canvas and to search for ourselves and for meaning. It was the time of discovery, use of metaphor - from nature to human's world, consciously and subconsciously, to develop vision that made us strong, believing that all this hard life was worth living. We needed time, being loyal to ourselves which means producing art out of fashions and short-lived currents.

We believed that our time hadn't come yet! One person from our village was helping us. He took many paintings, displayed them in his restaurant and was giving us dinners in exchange. The portions were small, but fourteen times delicious. The best was a dish with truffles. There was one place in the area with old oak trees. He went there with a dog, sniffing to find truffles. Some people trained the pigs to do the same. The restaurant was high class, people were coming from Marseille, two hours drive, to our small village, Tourtour.

Mr. Bajade was a great help for us.

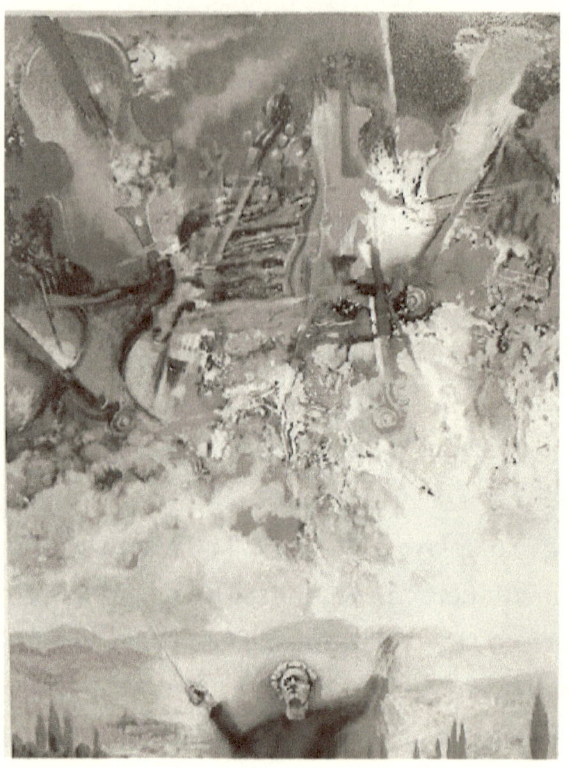

I asked, "What's behind the sky?"
He said, "The music."

CHAPTER 44

TIME OF GULF WAR

If you think your life is hard, it could be even harder.

One morning in 1991, the news came about the Gulf War. It was the day of our exhibition opening in Monaco at Latin American House. Not many visitors came. We were lucky to sell one big painting about the piano for 10,000 francs. It gave us a break for one month of living. Tourists stopped coming to the galleries. Even the one who painted chickens didn't sell anything. Nervously, Fitz started to smoke. I asked, "You stopped for one year. Why you started again?"

He answered, "Remember, I took airplane to France. Next to me, one man was smoking all the time, and I had to breathe this. My smoking habit came back, stronger than ever."

I had my head down. "You need to try again."

Every gallery started to sell out. We sold very little,

just for cheese and the wine. Mr. Bajade was almost bankrupt. He was so stressed out that he didn't talk to anybody.

But one day, somebody came to this restaurant - he liked our paintings, so he bought them all. He was Daniel Goeudevert, First Vice President of Green Cross International and former Deputy Chairman, Volkswagen Corporation. He saved Mr. Bajade's restaurant.

Fitz went to the doctor. His blood pressure was very high, so the doctor said some wine would relax him. We both needed to relax.

He decided to paint himself, very honestly done with some black paint flowing down like a symbol of threat for his life. But drinking the wine became a question of life and death. He was desperate to relax. We needed more protein. We had one last piece of fish left, and he refused to eat this by himself.

He said, "If only one nut is left, we'll divide it equally." The next thing, I heard him collapse. He fainted – that was terrible – time stopped for me.

We needed more wine to relax.

Alcohol can betray you without you knowing about it. One day, we went to the (cheap) restaurant, and we started to talk loud, with anger without knowing about what it was – alcohol talked for us. When we realized that we talked loud in Polish, that was terrible. We left the place quickly.

We came home, and I kept talking about something – actually, I was babbling. Suddenly I saw my husband cry. I never saw him crying. I was shocked. I became silent.

We decided to stop drinking – his cry was an eye-opener that there was something very wrong with us. He stopped instantly. For me, it was more difficult. I said to cut the wine gradually. At first, every other day and then every 3 days, every 4th day, and so on. It took me one month to stop completely. Fitz didn't interfere in my way. He understood that I was working on that. Life was still hard, but without wine, it was a new life. When you're drunk, you forget about love. Now we started to love each other again, and with respect for trying hard to change. We also remembered that we tried to fight alone for artistic destiny – coming here to Tourtour was part of it.

To give the most from our talents, without any compromises, without producing cheap and fast, we needed some support from powerful art lovers. But the hunger period continued, and the tourists didn't come yet. We had art for sell-out. Fortunately, with this mild climate, there's no season for vacation house owners. Sometimes they were visiting us and asked, "how much?"

Our answer was, "This is a sell-out, whatever you feel."

They didn't visit us every day. If they didn't, the next day was a day of hunger. Fitz said, "So there's no coffee left, only water for the morning."

"Whaaat?"

He continued laughing. "Just pretend the water turned into the coffee – just drink slowly, sip by sip."

I asked, "Any sugar left?"

"Yes," he said.

"So I'll add to the water."

"What are we gonna do after coffee?"

I heard sadness in his voice. "What else can we do? Go to the gallery and wait, hoping for somebody to come."

Sometimes somebody came, sometimes not. If somebody bought a little, we had the impression it was for helping us. We were grateful. We only asked ourselves, "When is it gonna end?" Something should happen – with this little touch of hope against hope.

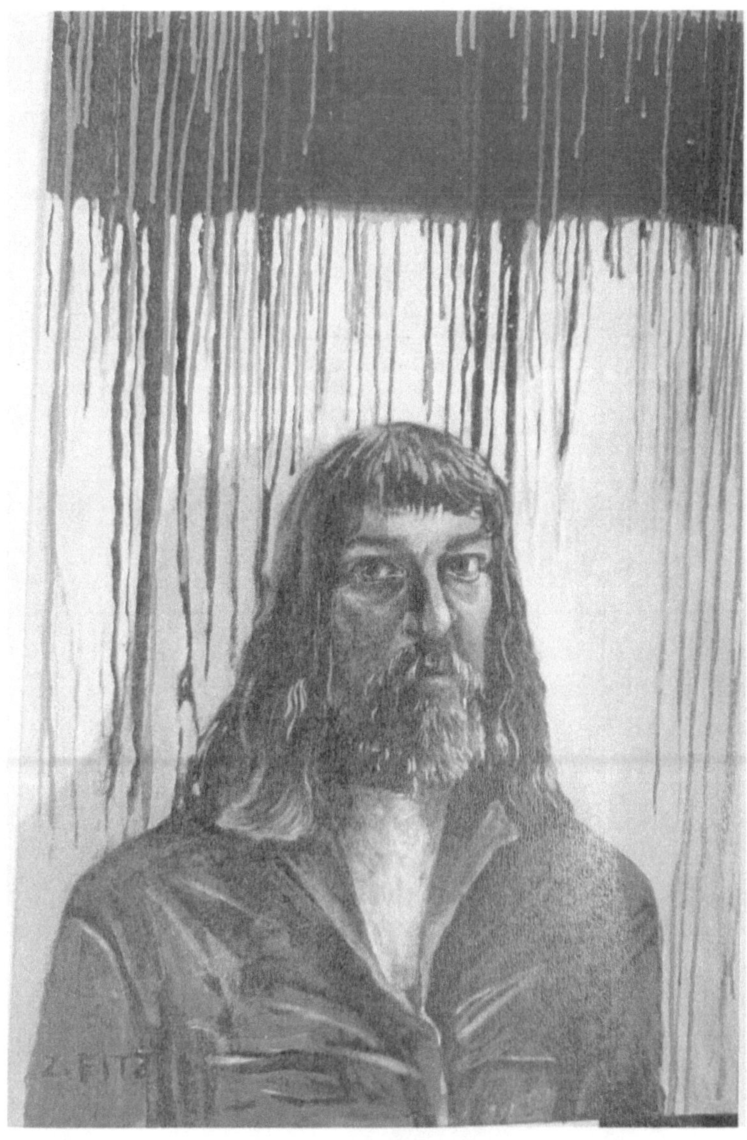

Zbigniew Fitz 1997 "Self Portrait" 46" x 36" ACR/CANV He was 44 years old.

CHAPTER 45

TOO GOOD TO BE TRUTH

We started to think over it. Fitz said, "Maybe we made a mistake. Maybe we should look for a gallery?"

I sighed, "Maybe."

He added, "Everything would be easier if we could paint full time and be represented by a gallery, but we always believed in being loyal to ourselves, not to produce out of fashions and short-lived currents."

I sighed again. "How to find a gallery that would give us freedom. We are still young, maybe our time hasn't come yet."

One day, we had visitors in our gallery who proposed a contract. This contract for a salary consisted of producing four paintings a month for one year, and then the contract would be extended indefinitely. "You're gonna work for us exclusively." The pair of our patrons consisted of one art consultant, a Parisian auctioneer, and Madame Macardi, from Monaco, who supplied the funds. 10,000 francs a month for living. They were both in their early thirties.

Fitz asked them, "There's nothing new in narrative art."

Macardi responded, "Doesn't have to be new – new is in individuality and skill. Most old masters were narrative. They were different in their individual profile."

Mr. Baniol added, "We'll give you great promotion, lots of important exhibitions, and you'll become well-known."

Fitz smiled. "For such a promise, it's hard to say no." After 8 months, they stopped sending us money. It was hard, since we became totally dependent on them. They came back to us after a year with a new contract and promise of the money, but we had to give them our paintings. If not, they were not gonna give us any money. We stupidly signed the contract, forced by our empty pockets and their promises of fame and fortune.

Right after we signed, they took every painting they could find in our house. Even work produced ten years before. They even went to the attic to see if there's anything there. They left in their truck full of paintings, and we stayed with a not so big check in our empty studio.

After a few months, we asked about the exhibition. Through her secretary, Mrs. Makardi told us about the exhibition, mentioning one gallery in Geneva. By curiosity, we tried to contact this gallery, but we discovered that the existence of this place was pure fiction.

The time passed, weeks and months, and finally we found that they specialize in selling estates, mostly deceased artists. They didn't do any promo – just sell cheap at the auction houses.

In our village, there was one good man, Mr. Michele Roux, a producer of Absolut Vodka. He helped us, found and paid a lawyer who was a specialist in such a case.

Finally, we were able to take back our paintings. It was the end of our fame and fortune adventure.

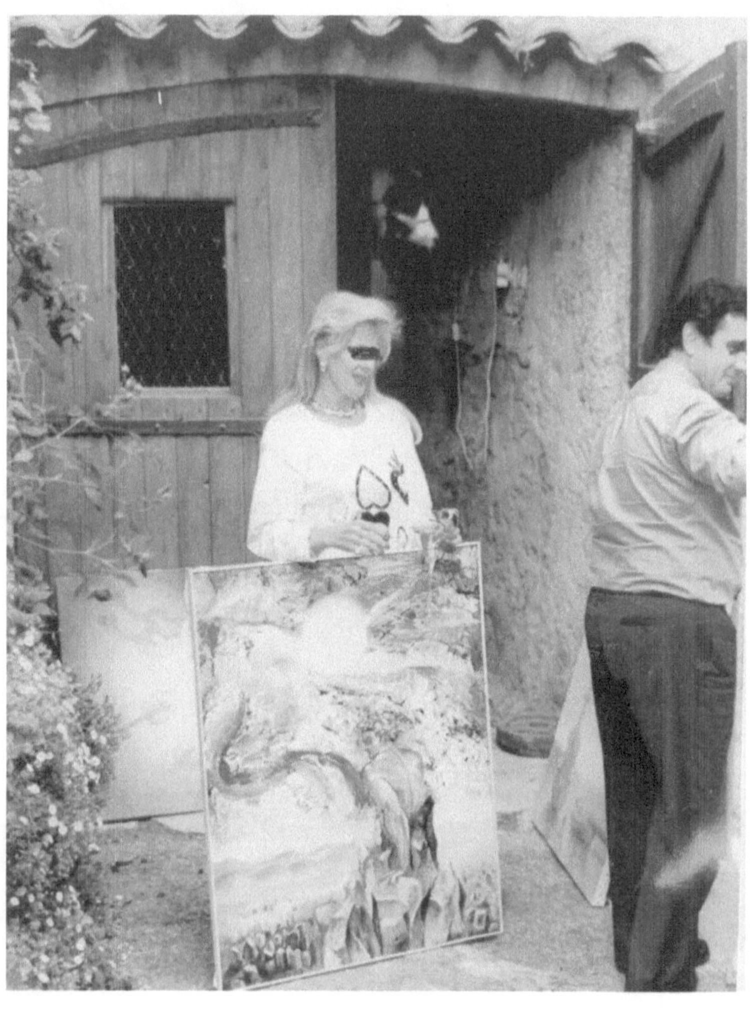

CHAPTER 46

TOO GOOD TO SELL

I woke up and burst into tears. Fitz turned toward me. "Why you cry, baby?"

I answered, "I want to come back to America. We made a mistake. We should never have come here."

He hugged me, held me close. "Don't worry, everything will be okay. I'll think of something. We'll do more exhibitions, and you never know what may happen."

I cuddled him. His optimism made me feel better.

Economic crisis in Europe created problems for many people, especially the foreigners. During the time of crisis, artists are the first victims because art is considered a luxury, not a necessity.

For us, the time of starvation came back. We were already affected psychologically by our past, and my fear became nightmarish before anything happened.

It is easy to imagine the empty refrigerator, utilities cut off and the question of how long our bodies can take the hunger. At least we had water. There were no jobs available during this time and certainly not to the strangers like us. I imagined in the case of extreme, I could go to our neighbors? Our pride was too strong, but we had made some friends, collectors from better times, and they kept buying from us from time to time.

It was impossible to organize any exhibition at that time, with one exception - a small gallery near Cannes, Mougins accepted our paintings. It was a kind of retrospective show including a few works from New York.

One event was significant for this period. A group of neo-Nazi, skin-heads came to see the exhibit. They noticed one of Fitz's paintings was critical of Nazi era, showing Hitler as one of the executioners. They chased Fitz through the whole village with chains, ready to massacre. Finally, the police showed up, and Fitz was saved.

As the Mougin Exhibit was coming to an end, a couple of Americans stopped. I was alone in the room when they asked what paintings from New York are doing there? They asked, "how much for this big one?"

I said, "This one is not for sale."

That was the best of Fitz's paintings. I was sure we were gonna need it in the future.

When Fitz came back, I told him about that. He was surprised, "Are you crazy? We don't have money for food. How did they look?"

I told him, "The man was tall like a giraffe, and the lady had a red coat."

This village was small. He found them visiting the church. He said, "this is my painting, and I decided to sell this to you." They came back to the gallery, paid 50,000 francs.

When they left, Fitz said, "You silly, silly, silly, but now we have money for living."

I smiled and said nothing. I felt his kiss on my forehead.

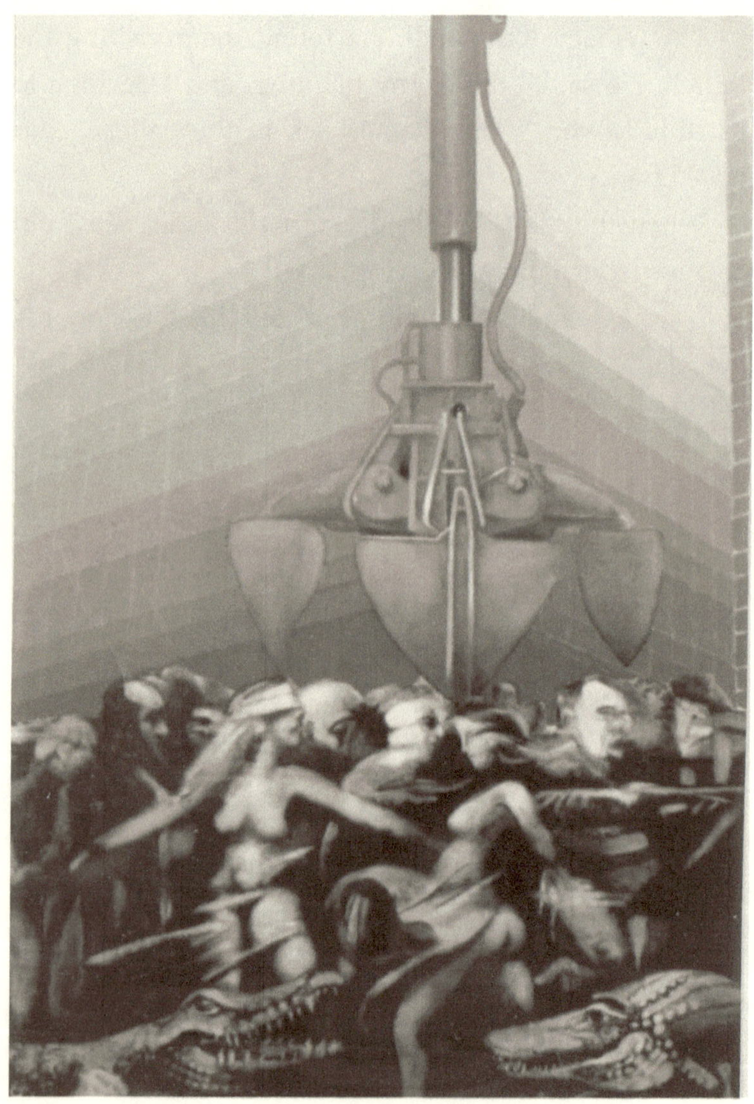

Zbigniew Fitz 1975 "New York Performance" 7' x 8'

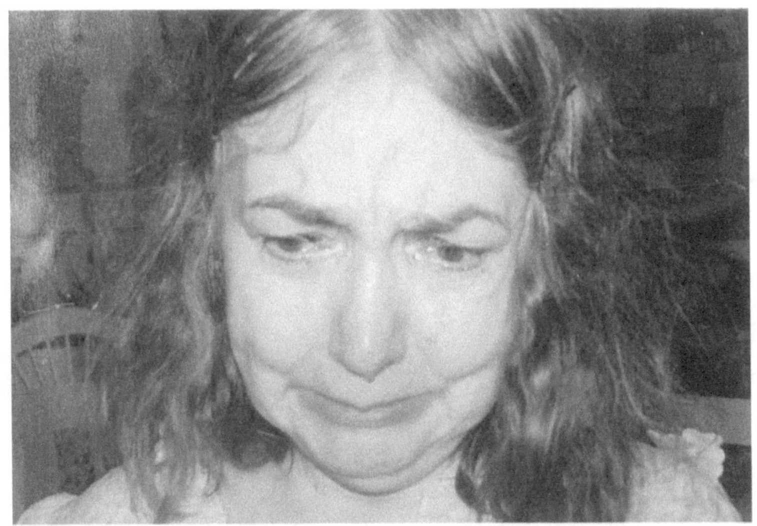

I Cry: "I want to come back to America"

CHAPTER 47

ANOTHER PROMISE

Mr. Parker Gomery came back to us two years later. He invited us to dinner and siad, "The reason I came to you is that I want to commission a series of paintings, "Passion of Christ". I'll pay you every two months just for living and execution. It should look the same style, like one person did it. After that, you should come back to the USA. I'll pay for that, and I'll make you a lot of exhibitions."

Fitz said, "We never did this kind of painting. Are you okay if we are not gonna do it for the churches, but we expect to have openings with forums in public places. It can be a discussion about different kinds of beliefs."

He said, "Ok, ok."

We were happy to come back to the USA - it felt like coming back home. Year was 1986. After we came back to the USA, the first thing our patron did was to exhibit in the church, in Santa Barbara, California. He was hoping to sell quickly. Next exhibition was at the DGA Theater Guild Film Festival for Religious.

There were many different church officials invited. Not any advertisement outside. Churches hated our paintings. Some of them said, "This contemporary, historical setting is too violent." "What is Christ doing next to Hitler?" "Why is Christ in a Concentration Camp?" It was taken down for a while.

There were no sales. Mr. P. Gomery was disappointed and angry at us because we didn't do this series more commercial. The article about us was in Hollywood Reporter [November 19-21, 1999] under the title "Inside the DGA Theater, a Portrait of Controversy" by David Robb. It was about how scandalous we were treated.

After the exhibition, our series of paintings was hidden in the basement of Pasadena Christian University at Brehm Center since 1999, never shown outside of Fuller Theological University with President Mark Labrerton. We did that before Mel Gibson.

Just for the memory of this series, we did seven versions of these paintings to keep it at our home. Since we had to work in the same style, we became very close to each other in art - that's what was my dream for so many years.

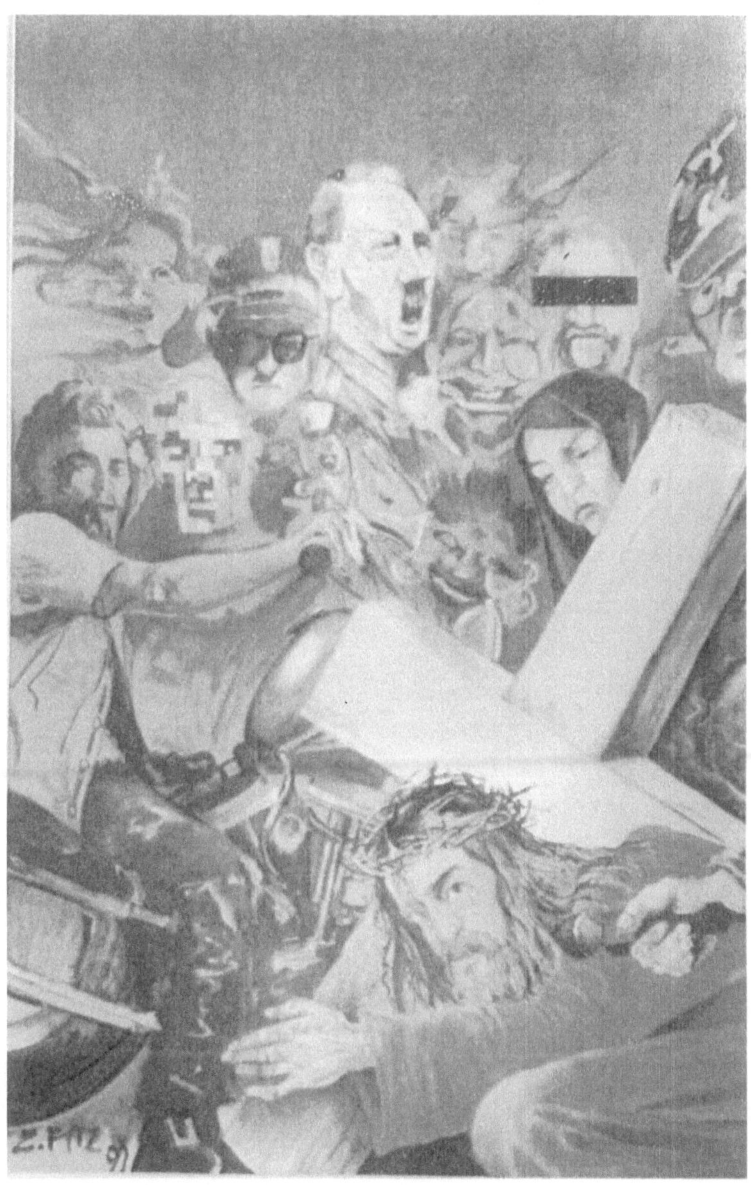

Zbigniew Fitz

CHAPTER 48

ARIZONA PERIOD

We came back to the USA in 1996. We made our home in Phoenix, Arizona.

The transparency of the air makes breath better. The sky is in itself a spectacular abstraction. During the monsoon, the rainy season, the sky is in movement, so colorful, it's like it is dancing. The one cactus is impressive, it's a saguaro, the most memorable of the desert. It's so majestic and beautiful that I wanted to hag. It stands upright, in a green column, 50 feet high. It can live as long as two hundred years. White, bug flowers in the spring are breathtaking, and it gives delicious crimson-colored sweet fruits. It is also a live water-storage tank, it's a giant cactus.

The desert is hot and dry. During morning hours, the air heats quickly to a maximum. About 2:00pm and at night, it could be 40 degrees lower. Rainfall is usually less than 10 inches annually. In the open sandy desert, a strong wind of 30 miles per hour, giving mini-tornadoes, desert devil, spinning, creating columns of air which sometimes rise to great heights, occurring most often in hot weather.

One day, I saw a desert devil going toward my way. By curiosity, I went toward it and Bam! I was inside the Devil. It became totally silent, totally empty. It passed quickly and left me with sand all over me - ears, nose, mouth - yucky! Watch your step where you go. Don't step on the tarantula, the largest spider. They are gentle, bite only if provoked but it's painful, not poisonous.

Once I found a scorpion under my pillow. The scariest thing to me was a rattlesnake. But they are nice enough to warn you by the rattle, giving time to escape.

One day, to my horror, I saw the cat near a baby quail. I scared the cat. Quail was hidden under the cactus. It was not easy to catch him. He had no more family. So we took him for the night. He was in the cage. For the day, he was free to walk in the apartment. He liked to sleep in my husband's beard.

We had our lunch in bed. He ate oranges, lemons, salads, etc. He was always checking out what we had for lunch.

One day, Fitz had a glass of red wine. So the quail came, tasted it and liked it very much. We were waiting to have fun, but he went to the end of the bed, stood there and got very sleepy. He woke up after two hours.

We never gave him the wine again. We loved the desert. We started to paint to sell. Colorful skies at sunset, very abstract. There was a once-a-year festival in Phoenix, but we were rejected. Our art was not enough western art. So, we made another try. We moved farther south, Bisbee. We took quail with us. Small town was very charming. There were many galleries. We rented a room and opened the gallery. Maybe we would not do that if we would talk with other artists. Most of them struggled.

Visitors were not rich. They were buying small, not expensive objects like soap, art craft, etc. Once again, we made a mistake.

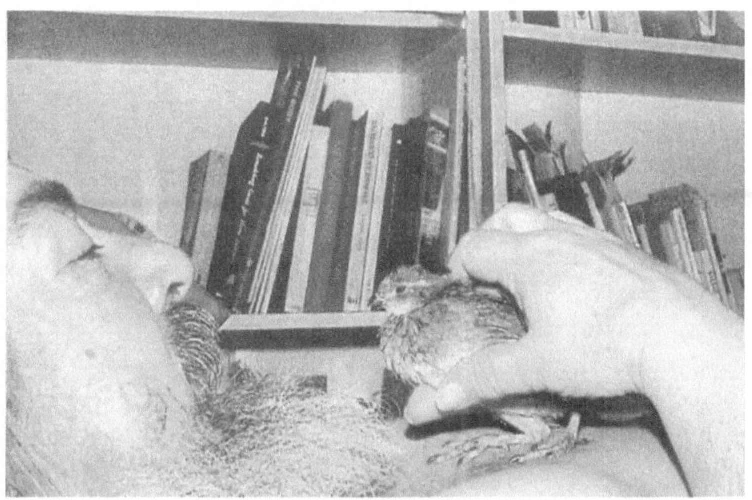

Baby quail liked to sleep in Fitz's beard.

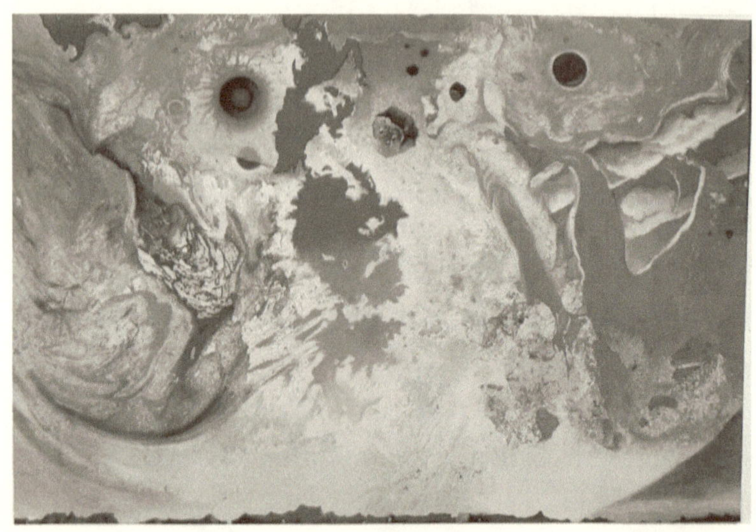

Zbigniew Fitz "AZ Sky Dance"

CHAPTER 49

DREAM STUDIO

Something New May Happen When You Expected Least

A small foundation from Rodeo, New Mexico, offered grants for talented, but not financially successful, people, like artists, writers and poets. This grant consisted of one acre of land, some building materials (like cement) and we decided to build the house, and a big studio, completely from scratch with our bare hands. It was a place in the middle of nowhere, very close to Mexico, windy and wildly beautiful. After the plans were accepted by the office, we started cleaning the land. The owners said, "You have your building material for free. You have rocks all over."

So after cleaning the land, we had to take a pickaxe and dig the trench, 18 inches deep, 15 inches wide, 60 feet long and 30 feet wide, the size of the house and studio. Before that, we had to moisten the ground to make it softer by water. The pipes with water were there.

Next, we took a wheelbarrow to bring the rocks from the field and make piles. They were helping us to mix the cement, put the rocks on the top of each other to make a wall. They were heavy. They showed how to clean the wall from the cement.

We wanted to have fun, so we took a rock or a brick and with cement, we created the faces, to build them into the wall. They gave us a temporary house, a mobile. They had storage, we could keep our paintings there, but some furniture, like a washer, we had to keep outside.

We had our quail with us. One day, I took him outside of the house. He fluttered on the roof and got scared, started to scream loud, like quail scream - kind of mew. I was afraid that an eagle could get him. I kept showing my hand and finally he came to me.

We were building one bed and planted brussel sprouts. It grew beautifully. When it was ready, I went to gather the plant. The brussels were planted thickly. I directed my hand inside. When I heard the rattle rattling, slowly I pulled back my hand, and I was safe.

After one year, we had our hands in pain. When we complained, they said, "Don't worry, it'll go away. Give it some time."

But it was not truth. After two years, the studio (it was 60 feet long with a greenhouse), was half-way. When we realized that, it started to destroy our hands.

Again, we had to leave the house to somebody else. It was a big decision. In the year 2000, we moved to Tucson, Arizona.

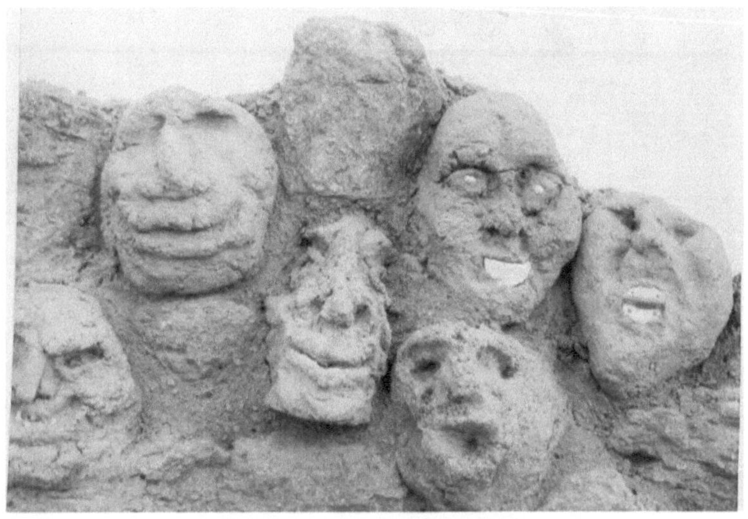

We created the faces, to build them into the walls. He dreamed about his studio to paint since many, many years. Emilia Fitz 2000 "Rebuilding America" 7' x 5' America, America - Dynamic, Spectacular!

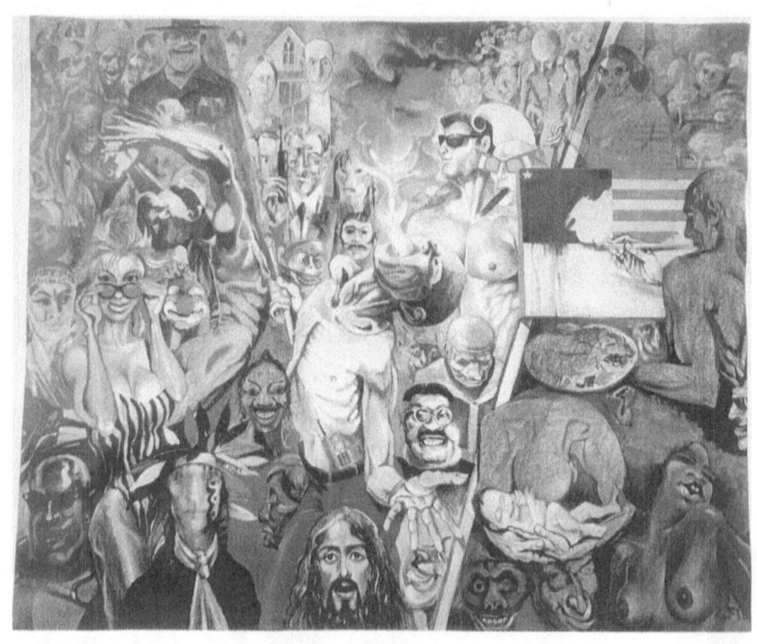

Z. Fitz "Painting America" 5 feet x 7 feet Acrylic/Canvas

CHAPTER 50

UNKNOWN FUTURE

We had never been in Tucson before. First thing we did, we stopped in the middle of downtown. We noticed that it was not too big, or not too small a city. We bought a newspaper and looked for the storage for our baggage.Next, we rented a room in the hotel and sat down looking for a job. If you are a painter, and that's all you do, you don't have any profession. We found a job in a factory making small boxes to pack something - the machine was set on a maximum capacity. It was stress for our hands and very painful. After one month, we had to quit even if the salary was very good ($12/hour). We were traveling through the suburbs when we saw the sign "Colossal Cave." We went there by curiosity. It was a very beautiful place. We asked if they have any job.

The Director said, "Yes, you can be a tour guide. We'll give you a text about what to say."

We felt, "What luck!", but it was a part-time job for minimum wage ($7/hour). One worker, a very nice woman, rented us a room. She was living alone, and the rent was very low. Also, it was very close to the cave. Our salary was very low, but I discovered that I had a very strong voice, a kind of soprano. I learned to sing Andrea Bocelli's "Ave Maria". The melody was so beautiful, people were giving me tips. Fitz had a radio with a battery and the tape "Amazing Grace" which he played in the Cathedral Room. He got tips for that.

He had breaks in the break room. The walls were made from rocks. It played on our imagination. We saw faces, so we started to draw them. The desert was so beautiful, we wanted to have our own house. We got the idea to ask for a mortgage. The man who once gave us commission work for religious paintings.

He accepted, lent us a $50,000 mortgage at 9%. It was $500 a month. With our salary, it was very hard, but we really wanted to have a home.

We bought a double-wide (used) with one acre of land. We made a garden, raised geese, chickens and ducks. There were many rats living under the prickly pear cactus, eating everything we planted.

In late spring, a family of quails were walking around. At least 10 babies followed the parents. It was very cute to watch. To attract them, I was giving them handfuls of seeds and water in a small dish. And the best was to attract hummingbirds with feeders. We liked the desert and the smell of creosote bush after the rain, or monsoon season, with spectacular lightning and all.

CHAPTER 51

9/11

September 11, 2001 was a beautiful day. The light of the sun was trespassing all things, putting us in a good mood. At 7am, we had our first coffee, looking out the window. Roses were still blooming in our dry desert yard, and we listened to conversations of quail passing by. It was a luminous morning, and we had to almost pinch ourselves to realize that we are living our dream. The TV was on, and we watched the news, almost ready to leave for work in the Colossal Cave.

We looked at the familiar image of two towers and suddenly experienced the shock and disbelief - time stopped and like in slow motion, we saw the plane penetrating one of the towers. We heard voices of broadcasters asking each other in disbelief, "is it really happening?"

After the second plane hit another tower, our mind's

clocks started to bend like in a Salvador Dali painting. We could not picture all those trapped inside - yet. Time came to go to work. At our arrival, we were greeted with sadness visible in all faces. We couldn't even say hello.

Nobody knew what was next, nobody felt secure. All our phobias and fears of war came back. We didn't have any family left. America was all we'd got. We felt like our home was attacked - it was like the ground was cut from under our feet. We decided to go to the cave alone, just the two of us. There was no electricity in the cave, so we took our flashlights. Because the cave was very dark, it may give an impression of descending to the grave. It was silent, the presence of another was assuring. In our imagination, we saw emerging from the darkness twisted figures and the rocks became faces. It was painful to watch all this. Masses of people falling down...down...down...

From emptiness to emptiness, nothing to grab, only a chorus of bodies, bent and crooked, swirling in a spasm of suffering. Streams of blood followed them until they blew to pieces, not possible to see where the face and the rest of the person were. Heads with lips wide open, gone stiff with unfinished words, where the fraction of the second became "forever." I heard Fitz whisper, "Horror...horror...horror." He had similar images to mine. Their tears in silence melted the rock's hearts, forming stalactites and stalagmites. One can shred bodies in pieces, but spirits can not be shredded. They belong to a different dimension, untouchable. They go up into the stars through fire or reason, and come back to dreams of those who cry after them - to console them.

There must be something that never dies - for loved ones, this assumption helps them to survive. Time doesn't heal, but memory is stronger than death.

There's something, somewhere, invisible particles, the presence that stays with loved ones – for eternity – it's deep inside of them…motionless…feel of love.

CHAPTER 52

SOLIDARITY OF ALL

We left the cave, the world was in a full sun and should have smiled - but it didn't. Visitors started to come. This time, we had visitors from all over the country and the world. The cave offered an unusual experience, but our guests didn't show much enthusiasm, everybody had their heads down.

The feeling of solidarity was coming from all. This time, we decided to go on the tour together. On such a day, the presence of another guide was assuring. Voice of Fitz (as a tour guide) was cracking from time to time, and it was not obvious if the pressive beautification of the rocks could talk to people. It seemed that everybody had similar visions. The cave is ½ mile long, divided by naturally created rooms. One of those rooms had incredible acoustics. It was a good place to stop and listen to the music played on a stereo system installed in this room. This time, the tour guide decided to play a fantastic rendition of Amazing Grace by Tramine Hawkins.

When the deep sound of her voice filled the whole cave, suddenly the well-kept emotions exploded like a volcano of tears. The river of sadness continued to flow down until the end of the song. The silence filled the room.

Spontaneously, everybody reached toward each other, hugging without words. We never saw this degree of emotion. People felt so close, and they came from all over the world and country. They shared one thing - humanity. They were on the same boat and their existence was precious and unique. They were all equal in life, love and death.

They knew that when they left the cave, it would be sunshine again. The feeling of being one came upon them and appreciation of this amazing life was greater than they could ever imagine. When we left the cave, we knew that our art will never be the same. When we were coming back from this dark, natural cave, I felt his warm hand holding mine, and I felt better because I was not alone.

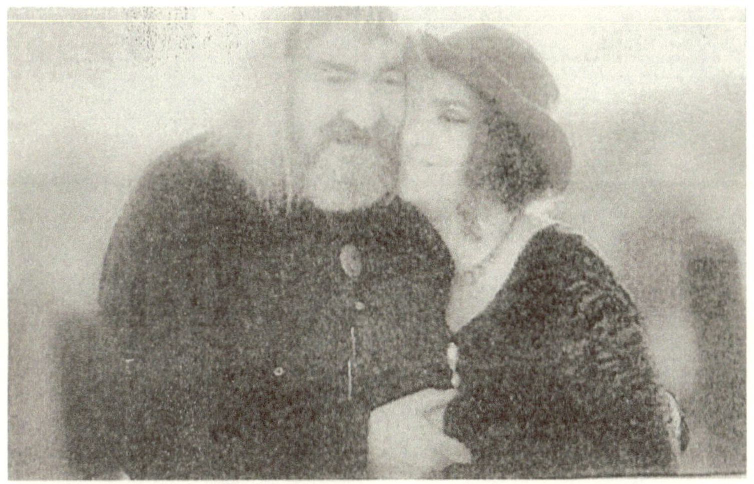

Zgibniew and Emilia Fitz

Emotional - Psychological Art.

Since 2001, we departed from native art, which became insufficient to express the deepness and complexity of our souls. Strong emotions became a link to our inside, to give stronger engagement to broader, intuitional perception and further mind development. To connect with the universal spirit our subconsciousness along with good skill worked for us to create and express the uniqueness of our personalities. There is intimacy of art where the soul of the artist is present in his paintings, in every touch of the brush, important or not. Future generations will feel that in their spirits.

CHAPTER 53

THE TURNING POINT IN OUR ART

The brain needs a hammer (metaphorically speaking.) The Artist's hand is not dead. Strong emotions (shock) are the ultimate push for creativity. In our case, it was the shock of 9/11/2001. That was the turning point in our art. The shock made a strong, emotional impact on our imagination. That goes deep to our inside, like it goes to the "memory" of genes and comes back to the surface, transformed naturally by the brain, creating forms of individual uniqueness.

Our psychological eye is seeing differently than the rational eye. When we observe humans in emotions, nothing stays in its own place. It's all twisting, swirling, moving in constant changes. We had to paint as we felt. When we observe human figures in different circumstances, confronting anxiety or dancing faces passionately in joy, reacting, living.

Picasso was right, replacing parts of the bodies, but

he stayed on a surface. We wanted to go farther, deeper to the person's inside. Our approach became psychological. Each touch of the brush was important, our skill gives us freedom of expression. All our deformations symbolized the observations about human nature. We learned about people and ourselves. We realized that paintings can be about mind development. To represent people of our time in a symbolic form.

Emotions can change our visual experience. Our perception of the world brings psychological expressionism. We saw that our creation has a good quality and we wanted to share that with others.

CHAPTER 54

VAN GOGH - MY REASON TO CREATE - Z. FITZ

Fitz made the article about Van Gogh - I just summarized this.

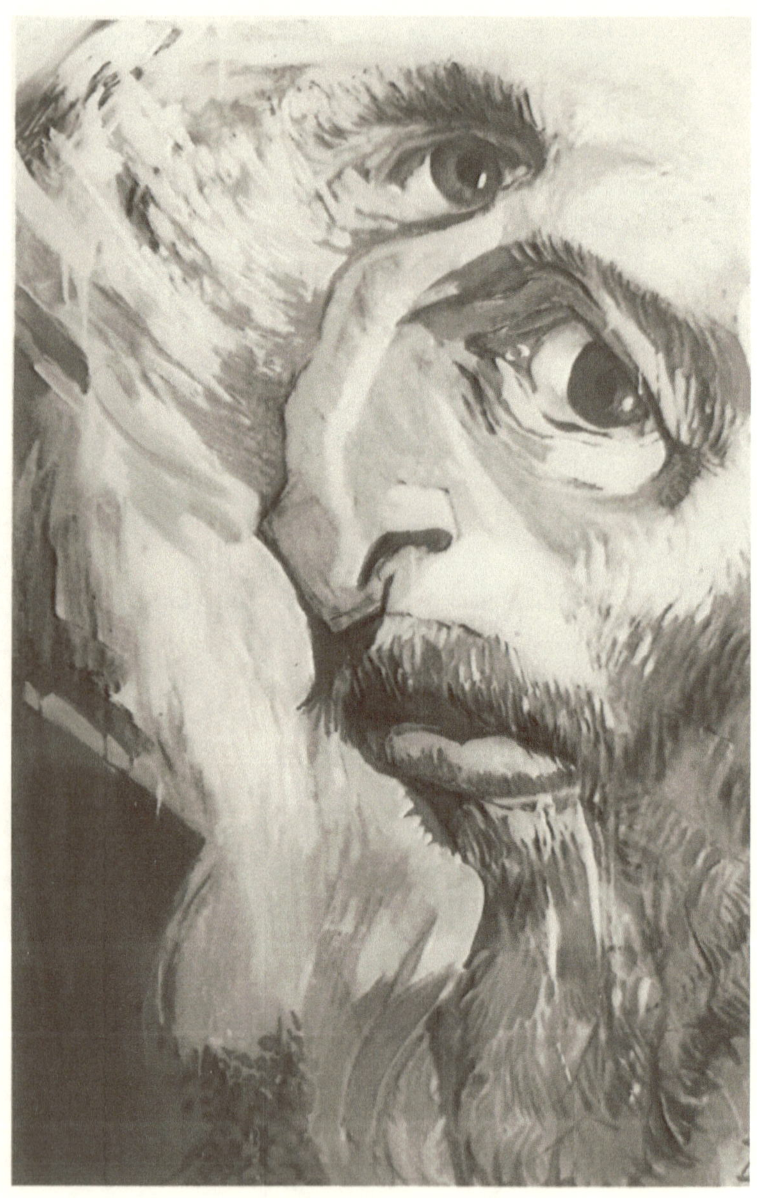

Zbigniew Fitz 2006 "Van Gogh" 60" x 48"

He "met" Van Gogh in very early youth. He identified with his struggles, abandonment by people. But he

wanted to paint for the light which was in him, like Van Gogh, to overcome inhumane situations alone. The light in him was worth living. With the eyes of his soul, he discovered the depth of the universe inside of his small room. His brush, obedient to his soul, moved to the areas where he could understand more. He knew his value. (His brush was extension of his inside, heart and his thoughts.) In his purity and innocence, he could not understand the indifference of people toward his talent. In sleepless nights, he asked the stars to rise above, be part of humanity's opus, true and eternal to shine over black ignorance.

Future generations will wipe his tears.

I stood before his painting: "This painting is the best you ever did - it came from the heart."

CHAPTER 55

STRAWBERRY

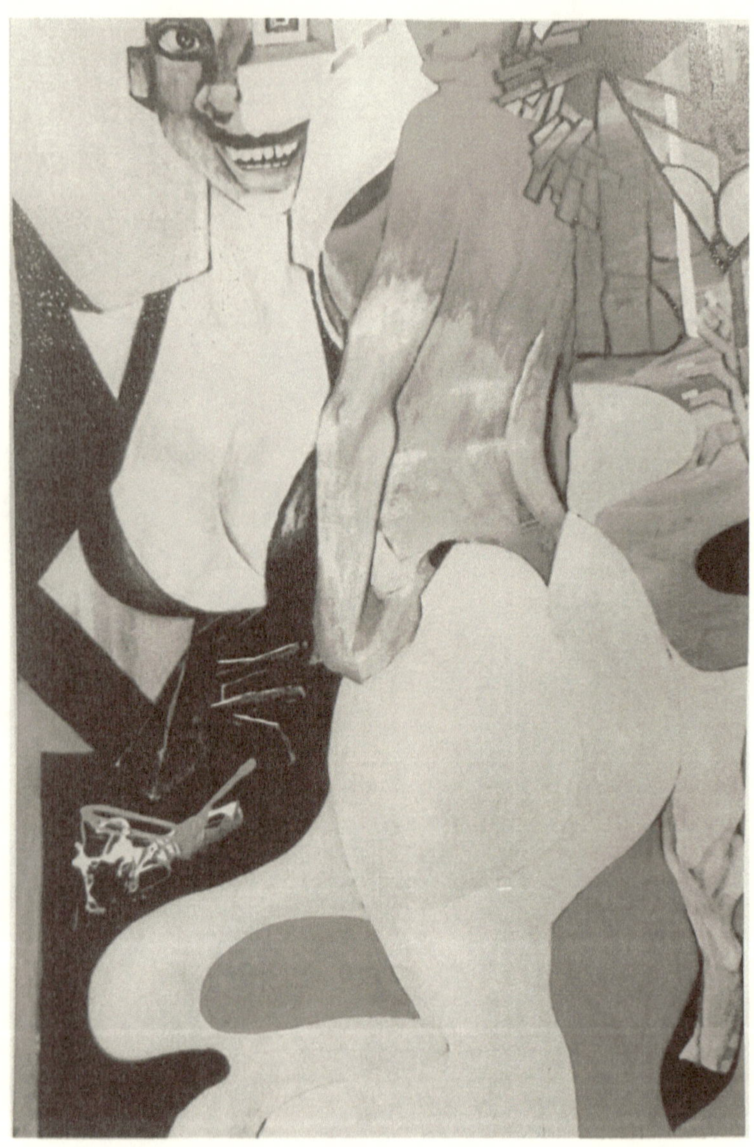

Zbigniew Fitz 2008 "Red Carpet" 51" x 38"

We didn't have enough time to paint, it was hard to make ends meet. But we tried to prepare our new way, to draw and search for forms. We made a drawing from a lipe model or mirrors. We had to do this for a long time until we could remember all of the body. After that, we could forget the study, invent a new figure. Because of our study, the invented figures were correct.

We could sit before an empty canvas, close our eyes, imagine some character and copy the image from our heads. When we search for forms, even the most trivial themes had spirituality in them - each brush stroke had the soul of an artist, that came from professional honesty.

Lunch time was a real time to relax. Fitz was preparing the meal, I was in the kitchen watching, and I saw that he was using too much salt. I told him, "you have high blood pressure. Salt is no good for you."

He said, "You nagging me."

I insisted, "You need to stop."

He answered, "You are annoying - get out of the kitchen - you'll see, you gonna like it."

I knew, for the little money we had, he was able to do almost a miracle to make a good chicken. I left the kitchen. The meal was delicious.

When he ate, he said, "We are almost out of the meat and herbs. Tomorrow we need to go to Trader Joe's. We discovered Trader Joe's was cheaper than anywhere else. They had a good policy, no pesticides.

It was eight miles from our home. When we were driving back, I fed him with strawberries we bought because he likes them very much. I chose the best for him, prepared the biggest. He saw this from the corner of his eye and asked, "Do you eat?"

I said, "Yes." I was lying. I just had a few.

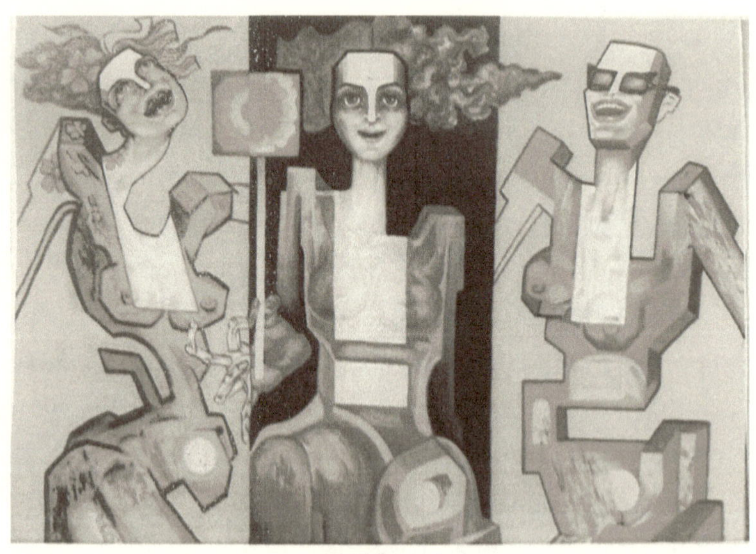

Emilia Fitz 2008 "Fashion Girls" Acr/Canv. 48" x 60"

CHAPTER 56

FIRED

H e just finished his "Self" when I was fired.

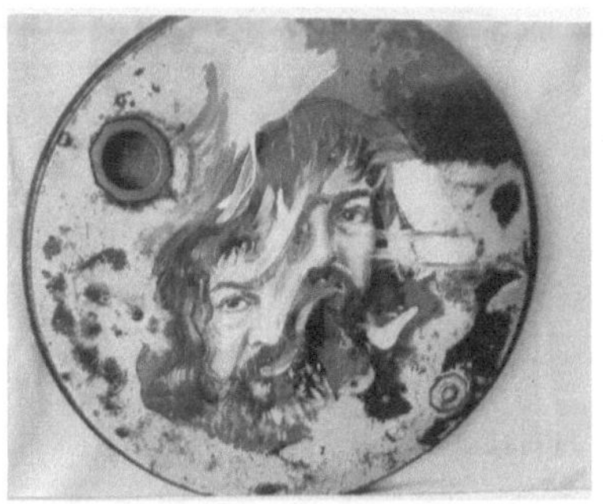

Zbigniew Fitz "Self" 2009 Collage/Paint/Metal Garbage Cover - "22"

They said that I'm singing too loud, my voice is too strong - it'll make stalactites and stalagmites break. We had to pay $500 a month for the mortgage. With a low salary, we were not able to make it without tips. So, we called the lender about it. He said, "You already paid $40,000 and only $10,000 left, so I can forget that."

We were very grateful. Now our life was easier. We had more time to paint, but Fitz had to continue to work. Now we painted, we talked, exchanged ideas, sharing. There was no competition between us. We cared about each other. Now our figures started to be twisted from happiness, full of emotions.

I mentioned one day, "I like Michaelangelo."

Fitz asked, "Why?"

I was replying, "because of the power of the human body. Adam represented the beauty of all Adams of the Earth."

Fitz asked again, "You mean the power of world creation?"

"Yes"

He answered, "Do your interpretation."

I paused. "Yes, I'll try to put feelings in his body."

Fitz stopped for a while. "And I'd like to take picture of you, but no make-up or not even brush your hair."

He was a good photographer. I liked my face very much - very inventive.

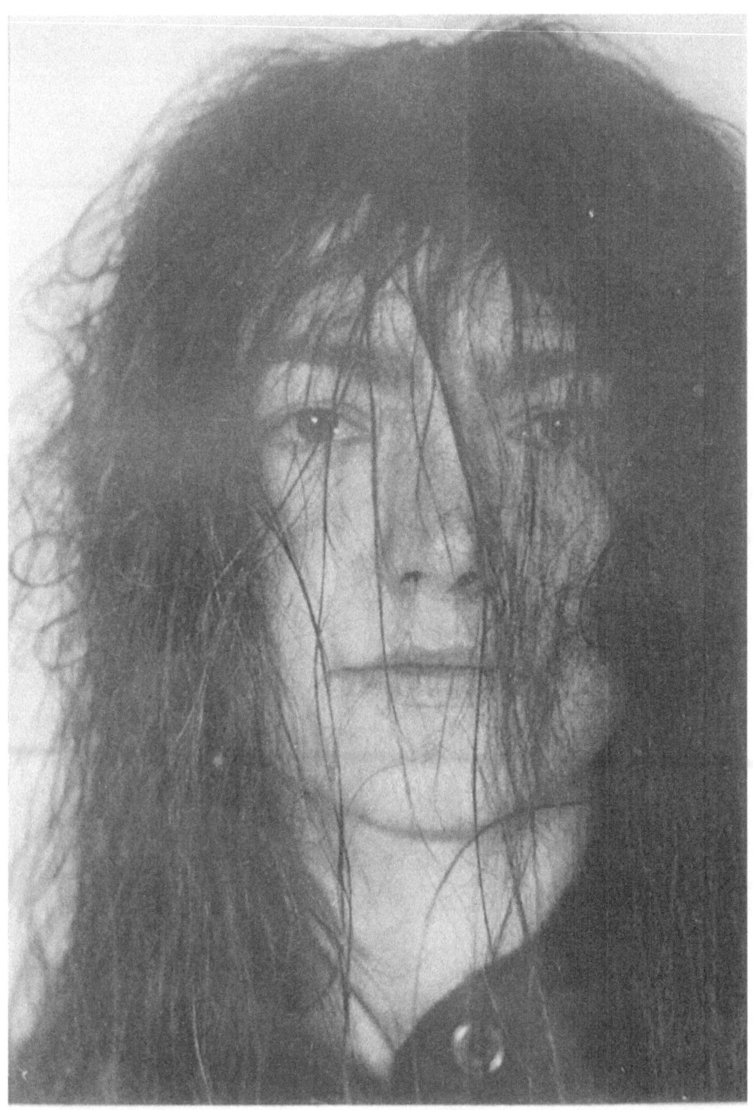

Zbigniew Fitz Photo of Emilia

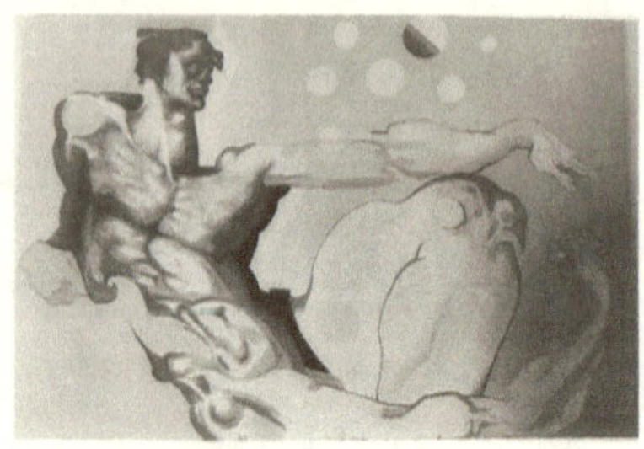

Emilia Fitz "Adam After Michaelangelo" 48" x 60"

Learn from Masters and add something on your own.

I started to make drawings for my Adam. After I finished the painting, he praised me.

CHAPTER 57

OUR BEST TIME

We were totally immersed in paintings every day. We cared about each other, exchanging ideas, talking, asking who wants to do what - shared.

We made drawings from a live model, usually from a mirror, observed from nature. One day, we were watching TV. A group of women did aerobics. Fitz got excited. "Look. Look."

I asked, "What? What?"

He said, "I am gonna paint that. I'm gonna do an allegory to the human activity, going fuller, with all intensity, until changing from, surpassing themselves. It's about life itself. It's a pulsation of life, instant movement, eternal ecstasy of existence. It is changing endlessly in its own swirling, deformed. Nothing can reflect it better than the form we are doing now. It's so promising in our art development. This intensity of movement, it's a necessity of living. Look, she's gasping for air, one leg strongly, quickly jumping toward, to be followed by the other, her beautiful big bosoms joyfully moved with music, the rhythm of life dancing with the rest, like a child who must move almost constantly with a smile to the future."

Face is the most expressive, turned upside down in an effort to breathe desperately, nose wide open to bring more air, she's about the dynamic and beauty of health, to live long, maybe to be young forever?...

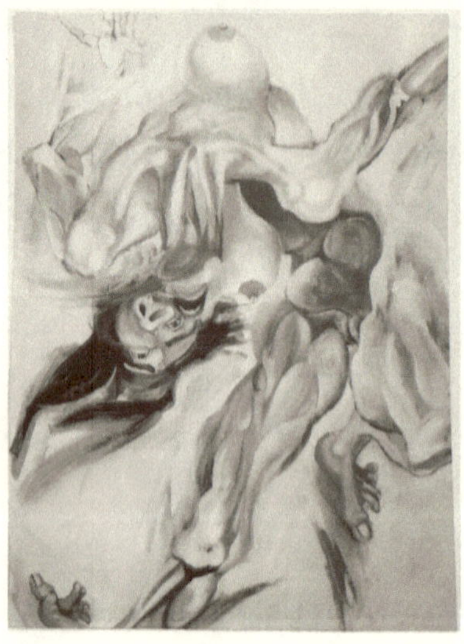

Zbigniew Fitz 2006 "Aerobics" 72" x 48"

CHAPTER 58

"NO SHAME OF YOU"

I was just pouring out a glass of liquid paint, gray, on my canvas. Suddenly, I heard voice of my husband behind my back. "Do you know what you are doing?"

"Not yet," I replied. "This time I wanted to be spontaneous."

"So you don't have any idea what you are doing?"

"No."

He said, "Remember, after 9/11, our perspective is different." He continued, "Spontaneous doesn't mean chaotic. Empty brain without any plan of organization - you'll be lost at the end."

"And?"

"You need some kind of inspiration. Correlation between feeling and thinking is important for creativity, two things condition each other. You need to start again!"

I jumped from the chair. "No, you gotta be kidding. I'm not gonna change."

With his quiet voice, he insisted, "I don't want to be ashamed of you."

"No, no and no." I started to cry.

He said, "you have to start again." I went to the bedroom, came back with a sheet and made separation between us. He took the sheet down to the garbage. "There will be no separation between us. Just try, and you'll see. I am right." I was sitting in silence, sulky. He broke the silence. "I have an idea. Let's go to the store (Trader Joe's), maybe you'll see something. Inspiration comes from emotion toward figure. Their humanity is your humanity. You'll start to draw the model and it will be your interpretation."

I finished his thought, "I know, I know. I'll put order by rhythm of planned composition."

"Yes, the meaning of the model is about the meaning of yourself. And you'll dig for the essentials of things until you'll be in a state of ecstasy."

"Let's go."

"We'll buy strawberry?"

"No, it's too expensive. We'll buy chocolate."

He looked at me. "Now, smile, please, pleeeeease." And he kissed me in the forehead. He hugged me, looked deep in my eyes with his smile. I could not resist that, so I smiled back. I knew that after arguing, the night was gonna be very passionate. I smiled in my mind, threw my arms about his neck, and it felt good.

CHAPTER 59

SAATCHI GALLERY

When we came back from the grocery store, I got very excited. "Listen, I saw extraordinary woman, tall with big bosoms, like two apples. She was very pretty, emotional, talking so much, her moods were changing constantly from anger to laughter. It was weird."

Fitz answered, "You need to have a total trust to yourself, accepting what's coming from your inside, no matter how weird it may seem."

I said, "Looking at her, I became emotional."

He reacted to my words, "The art is powerful, like a power of your emotions. Feeling and thinking depend on each other, and the essential will come during the process of execution."

I couldn't stop my excitement. "She was incredible and beautiful. She was talking fast, her big, pretty lips were running in a circle around itself. When something catches my eye, it provokes me on an emotional level first. Her hand was the reflection of her being, each finger had its own expression adequately to the meaning she represented."

Fitz added, "Grab your mirror fast and start drawing. It's very promising."

I posed, "I can only deal with one moment. The image is different from the words. With the words, you go around in many ways, but image has to replace a thousand words, freezing the essence in time."

Fitz finished my thought, "And now your instinct will play a crucial role, expressed metaphorically. That's a mystery of talent." When I finished the painting, 7′ x 6′ size, he said, "That's one of your best - it's deeply felt." And he added, "I'll put it on Saatchi Gallery online." It felt good.

CHAPTER 60
VALLEY FEVER

In Tucson, we had one acre of land, full of flowers. Rabbits were eating irises and rats were living under the prickly pear cactus. We didn't want to cut cactuses because those blooming in the spring were breathtaking, some yellow, some red, fruits were edible if you know how to get rid of spines. I wanted to fence our area. I started to set posts in the ground. There were big rocks inside which I didn't see. Suddenly, I felt a sharp pain in my neck. I went to bed with trouble. The pain was so strong that any position in the bed was not right. I couldn't make any move.

I didn't want to take any strong painkillers, so I laid down and tried to listen to the pain, ordering it to stop - sometimes it worked. Fitz was feeding me with all his love, gently. In about two months, it started to feel better. Another surprise was waiting for me. I woke up with a high temperature. Slowly, it continued to go up. Fitz went to the pharmacy to ask for advice.

He came back, opened the door, made the signal with his finger toward him, "Get dressed quickly. We have to go to the emergency room. You may have pneumonia."

At the emergency room, I had to wait for two hours while my temperature slowly kept going up. Finally, when I saw the doctor, he said, "You are lucky you came on time, because pneumonia started to go to the other lung. If ever it would go (inflammation) to your blood, you would be dead."

After many tests, the doctor didn't know why I had this. At one point, she said, "You have lung cancer." Fitz gave me the look with such love. I couldn't stay in the room. I ran out not to cry before him. Finally, the result was that I had Valley Fever. It's a fungus living in the lungs, not contagious, but it makes you feel weak. Pneumonia made me cough so often for a long time that I lost my voice.

I used lots of papers to communicate with Fitz. All this happened in the best time of our creation.

CHAPTER 61

RAGE

Most of the time, I was in bed, down with a fever. I felt helpless and worthless. I didn't say anything to my husband. He had enough problems. One day, I wanted to tear my body to pieces. I bend down transforming myself into the grimace of huge anger. No one could see my feelings. I felt like squeezed raisins or misshaped like a burning newspaper, my hands in twisting spasm. Face and body became smashed pieces of paper almost disappearing in my own state of destruction.

This stage would kill my spirit if it wouldn't transform into the stage of creativity. I decided to paint my anger to ease my pain. I started to draw in bed, lots of sketches, looking for ideas to express these feelings. The next step was to take a mirror and study my body. I did grimaces and twisted my naked body to learn, observing the model I became. I had a terrible need to "talk" about my drama. I was going on with doing the drawings for many weeks to come. After many weeks of preparations, I was ready to paint on big canvas.

It took several months to complete. That was the copy of my imagination. That cured me. The power of expression in art is that one becomes somebody from nobody. These kinds of feelings are the most private one can have. But I also knew that what is the most authentic would give the most powerful art.

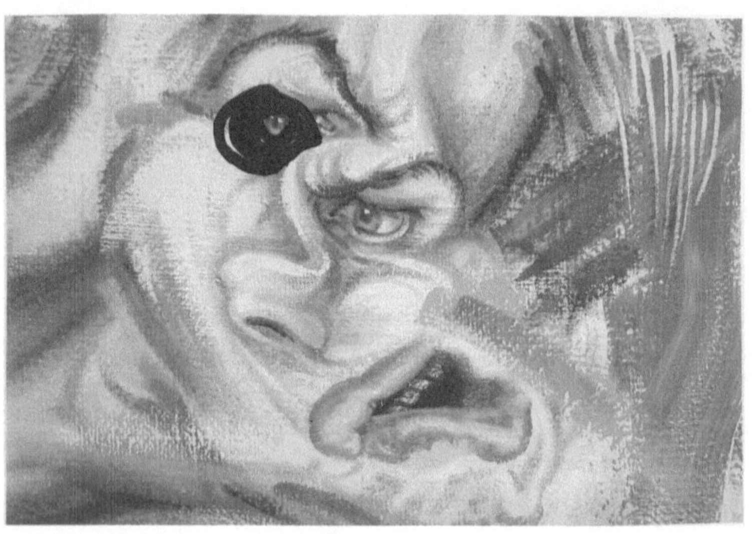

Emilia Fitz 2006 Detail from "Rage" 6' x 7'

CHAPTER 62

SAVED

It was the year 2008. My voice hadn't come back yet. When Fitz said something, I had to write my answers. One day, he woke up. "I have something important to say. We need to save you. You can't get Valley Fever and Pneumonia again. We need to change the climate, go where it is humid." I was touched.

The Arizona climate was good for him, but he wanted to sacrifice himself for me. We sold the house, had to give up quail, and came to South Carolina because it is humid and cheap. We bought the house from the bank, spent lots of money in renovations, made dream windows - skylights and bought tools and flowers for the garden. After two years, we realized the house had black mold and dangerous cracks on one side. We sold this one and bought foreclosure in Great Falls, a small town with 1,000 of population. The house was big and again, smelled bad with black mold. We didn't realize that before.

During that time, we started to send letters to the galleries and kept getting the same answer. "You don't fit."

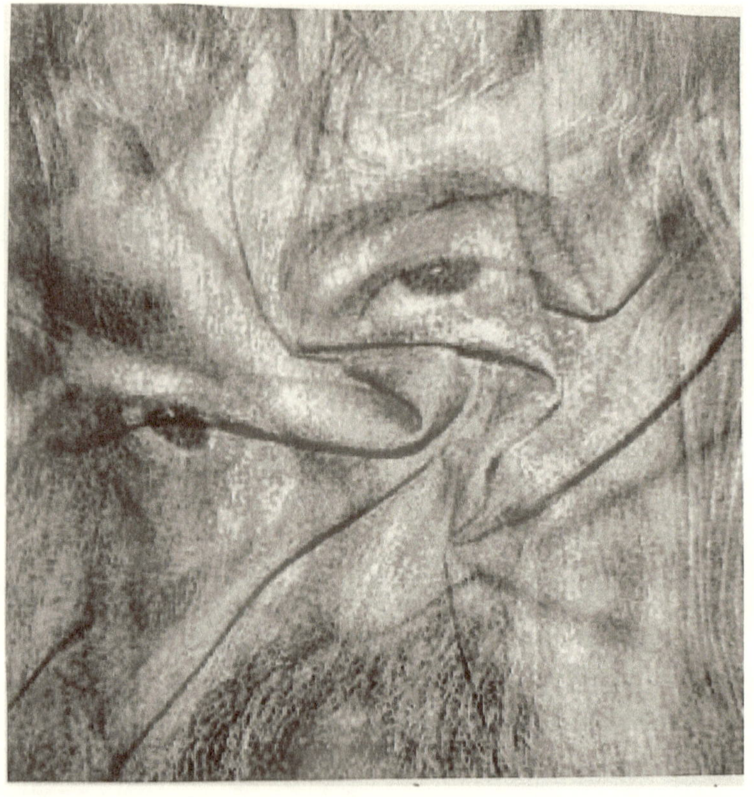

Zbigniew Fitz "Self"

We didn't know that you have to fit to do good art. Most of the masters didn't fit. Fitz started to do digitally manipulated photos. It took him three years, but that didn't fit either. He had a beautiful idea of juxtaposition or different textures of tree bark on the human body. For health reasons, we had to sell the house again and bought another foreclosure. It was a suburb, six miles from a small town. We prepared the garden, bought one track of flowers, tools, fences and renovated the house, which was in bad shape: no floors, full of cockroaches.

It took time and money, but I was always full of hope in the beginning. We started to question when each time in the garden we got headaches. We asked each other, "There must be something wrong with this place." He checked online and, to our horror, there were people producing meth (methamphetamine.) That's why it smelled like rotten eggs and also the traffic was terrible, even at night, very noisy.

We started to think about changing again. This time our dream was Ashville, North Carolina. We always liked mountains. Fitz started to learn better writing in English, to do the book. He was always very ambitious. He wanted to do something dystopian, something meaningful. He was sitting before the computer for many hours. When I pushed to do breaks every 30 minutes, he said, "I can't concentrate with breaks so often."

Quote: "The opposite of love is not hate. It's indifference."

Elie Wiesel (poet, writer, Holocaust survivor)

CHAPTER 63

GOT TIREDER

Slowly, after years of stress, we started to be tired, irritated and jumpy, but we cared about each other.

One day, Fitz went outside. I glanced by the window and saw him smoking. I called him home. I was very angry, "You assured me that you don't smoke anymore." I smashed the dish to the floor and left outside.

After 10 minutes or so, he opened the door and said, "Come home, you'll get cold." I came and saw he cleaned the broken dish. "I'm sorry, I'll try again and again. The habit is very strong."

I said, "Remember, you promised."

"Yes, my love." He added, "You are a good person, but when you are angry, there's nothing worse than to see your face." I smiled.

He asked, "Do you feel better now?"

"Not really."

"Do you feel ashamed a little?"

"Yes, it doesn't feel good."

"Come here." He hugged me. That felt good. I kept convincing him to go to Asheville. "You don't have to try so hard, I already said OK." I guess I was stupid, I should know him better. He added, "Don't complain every day about something. We already know our situation."

"I'll do my best." I kept worrying, "You'll publish your book on Amazon, only well-known people selling the books."

He was laughing, "You started again, let me try." Once he said, "don't scream."

"I'm not screaming."

"You can scream in whisper. I can feel your anger. For me it's loud."

"I'm sorry, I sometimes have a bad temper. I'm too emotional."

"So try to overcome yourself."

"I'll try."

"Now, kiss my cheek."

Emilia and Zbigniew Fitz Artist's Statement:

Why do we have to do art? For us art is the answer to the question, "To be or not to be."

To define our identity is to mark our existence. To do something good, conscientiously, is the quality or need of human beings. Doing art is one of the ways of exercising such a possibility. Art could be anything, but also it could be everything. We can play like children, or we can look at the mirror and ask fundamental question: Who we are? Sometimes we use unexpected tools to dig for the mystery of human beings. We know that certain parts of us can be extracted from the darkness of our beings by subconsciousness - those sensitive, hard to define areas, can come out in metaphorical ways.

One of these ways is to paint. We can touch the unknown in us or dramas of reality around us. We can also dream, escape from reality or enhance the positive part of it. Our search for ourselves is the work in progress.

CHAPTER 64

OLDER - BETTER

With time passing, the older he got, the better person he was becoming. He was everything I ever wanted. He was so positive, hopeful in any situation, very gentle, full of wisdom, talented, thoughtful, civilized, concessive. If ever I wanted something, for example, one more flower for the garden, even if we didn't have much money, he would buy it for me. He loved peace, never wanting to harm anybody. I had heaven on earth. He was cooking every day.

If ever I was tired, he was saying, "Stay in bed. That may be Valley Fever waking up in you." He was bringing a meal to my bed. It was always delicious, even very simple. He knew the right herbs to use for chicken. He never argued or talked back. Never ignored me no matter what not important or stupid thing I said. If ever he went to the store alone, always called, exactly the time he promised. We had such a compatibility, when I started the sentence, he could finish it by telepathy. He was very sensitive and attentive. He was tender, heartily, warm, affectionate, and mindful. If ever he saw my face not happy, he asked, "Are you okay?"

He would share everything with me, even his ideas for paintings. We completed each other, had the same value system in life and art - after 50 years together, we became one.

Even if we had different characters from nature, like I was more impulsive, he was quiet, able to bring balance between us, accommodate the differences, disputes, and bring humor. He liked practical jokes. Once I left the room, I went outside. When I came back, he pressed the door so that I could not open it. I could hear his giggle on the other side of the door. He also liked dry humor. He said something stupid, and from the corner of his eye, he could see if I paid attention to his words. Even getting older, he was always handsome. One can see this from his self portraits very accurately done.

Recently, I found a little diary from May 1970. I started with, "Why I cry?" It was in Paris. It said, "My love, you went to 'Place Dutertre' to do portraits of the tourists. Did you eat anything? Are you tired?"

I went there to see him. There he was, sitting alone, waiting. No tourists came, so he didn't make any money. I said, "don't worry, tomorrow will be better.

Come home, take some rest, some piece of cheese and one bottle of wine left."

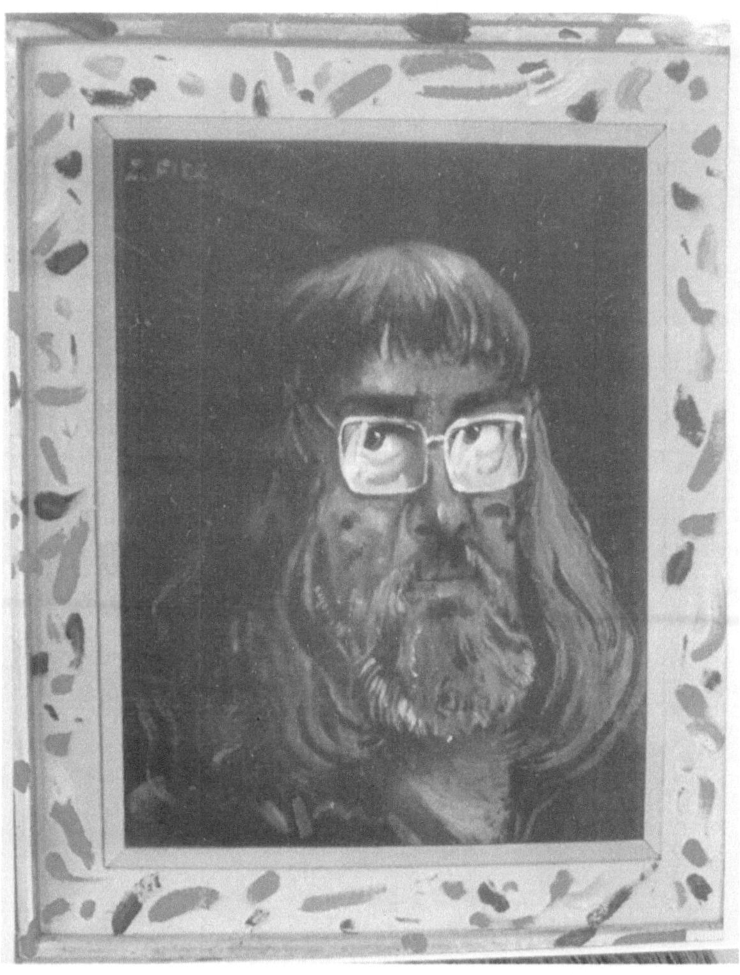

Zbigniew Fitz 2009 "Self-Glareing" 19" x 15"

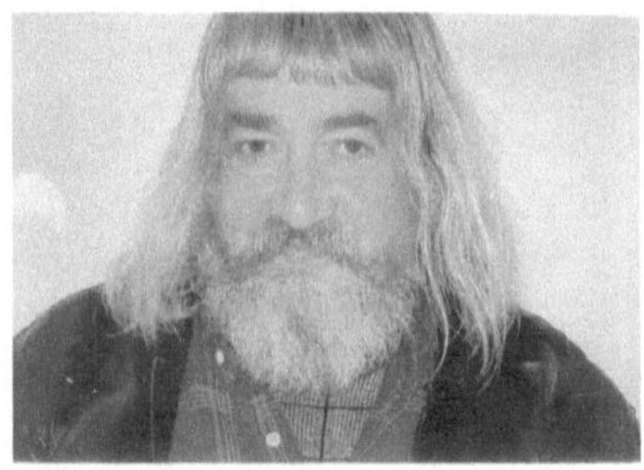

He smiled. So why do I cry today? He just did his self. His piercing eyes penetrate our soul. Could he feel that indifference is gonna kill him? He was seeking for the tiny dot of hope until the end.

We became a symbol of what lifetime friendship can do for art. We did good art. You don't have to fit, just create for future generations. Disinterested. Any conscience now in this generation? My tears answer that. But he was positive. September 4th, he was smiling, to go to the grocery - Trader Joe's

CHAPTER 65

LAST WORD OF THE DAY

It was September 5, 2014.

We went to Trader Joe's to do our monthly supply of food. It was one hour to drive. I broke the silence, "We are each 71 years old. What is our achievement?"

Fitz replied, "We got a skill, and skill gives freedom of expression."

"Yeah," I said. "Your self portraits are very good."

He added, "Your self is good too."

I continue, "We have several paintings starting from the 1960s."

He concluded, "shown in chronological way will show the progress of our brains through art."

I looked at him. "Not all our art is serious."

He answered, "Even in the most trivial themes, there's a spirituality - each brush stroke has a soul of the artist."

I finished his thought, "I know, I know, that comes from professional honesty. Some curators said that our art is powerful."

He added, "Yes, that comes from emotions."

I pointed out, "your eyes see differently when on camera."

"Yeah," he added. "Distortions of the human figures enhance psychological expressions."

I remembered, "Some art critics said 'Your art is inventive - your art is psychological expressionism'."

He looked toward the horizon. "We didn't waste our life." It felt good when he said that. And he glanced at me. "Now I have to do a book to improve our situation." He was very excited about that. When we came back from the grocery store, there was a thunderstorm and the computer was broken. He got very stressed. All his preparations for the book were destroyed. When I saw him by the window, his face was in distress.

I said to him, "Don't worry. Let's go to the "Gun and Pawn" store. We have $100 left." So we went there. They had a used computer - it worked well. He was relaxed.

That night, before going to sleep, he used the name he invented. He took my hand tenderly and said his last word of the day, "Cushca."

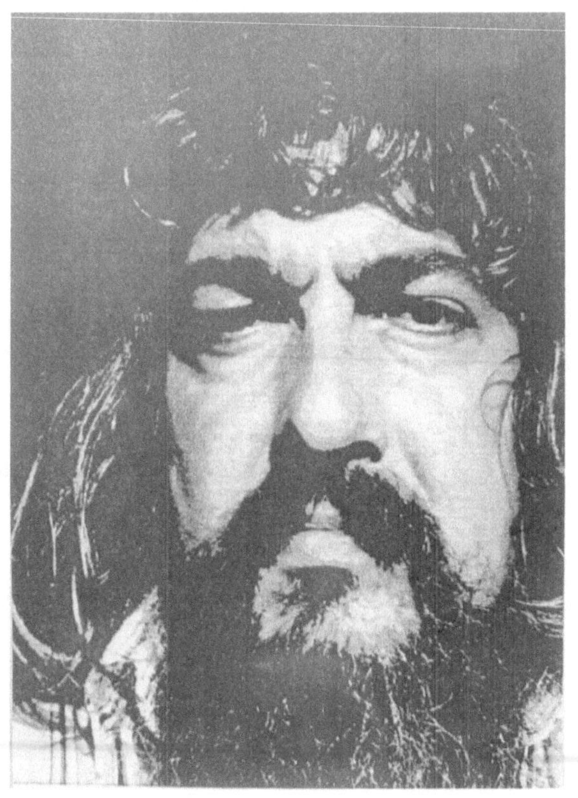

CHAPTER 66

SEPTEMBER 6, 2014!

It was September 6, Saturday, early morning. I heard Fitz going to the kitchen. I thought he went to get coffee. I went back to sleep. Suddenly, I heard a big house crack - it was a big sound. I jumped from the bed asking, "what's happened? What happened?"

In a second, behind my back, I heard a sound coming from Fitz, rattle like, like he was suffocating. He was on his right side. I ran to him. "Are you okay?" No answer, but I don't know how he turned to my voice. I didn't know he was dying.

How much you had to love somebody to turn toward him in your last breath. I started to do CPR, to press his chest and called 9-1-1. I pressed his chest until my hands started to be in pain, but emergency people came in 10 minutes. I took his jeans and denim shirt. I was sure he would be back home soon.

Our neighbor came with us to the hospital, and we were waiting for several minutes. When the door opened, a group of doctors and staff came. I saw their faces in sadness. The doctor shook his head. "No, he died. It was a massive heart attack."

I became flabby. The woman took my arm, but I didn't realize I was walking toward the home. It was unreal. I was in a different dimension, like a Twilight Zone. Everything was fluerblear, foggy. Time stopped. I was frozen. In a few minutes, I found myself in an empty house. The silence was like death, only the clock was "tick-tock, tick-tock, tick-tock…"

I looked to my right side, the pillow was empty. I asked, "How can I pass the night?" I didn't sleep at all, I could not process what just happened.

In the morning, I had an idea that maybe he's gonna wake up. Sometimes it happens - I was in denial. It helped me to pass the second night. The next day, I was staring at an empty wall or had my head down immersed in my darkness. The air was still, nothing moved. The silence was crushing, depressing, over-whelming. I was totally devastated.

This silence… this silence….

Suddenly, I saw something moving. It was a cock-roach. Finally I was happy to see life. I didn't kill him. I was indifferent to anything. Frozen. Death didn't ask my opinion. No more time for reflection. My knees talked on my behalf - they bent by themselves and my heavy eyelids looked up with the last energy, seeking for hope. The slightest chance to make sense against all odds, begging for God's existence.

I didn't sleep, didn't eat for weeks - I couldn't swallow anything.

One night I was sobbing into my pillow, and I got up and went to the kitchen. I started to cry, louder and louder. I screamed for a long time until I lost my voice. I whispered, "God, God, where are you?" With no answer to my distress, I took a knife and directed it to my chest fiercely, but it missed, went to the table and curved. Probably, in my subconscious, I didn't want to die. Killing, any killing, was against my beliefs. I kept whispering, "God, where are you?"

When I saw I won't be able to answer that, I just asked, "If I want him to exist?" With every fiber of my being the answer was, "Yes!" If God exists, my Fitz, his spirit is alive. But I wanted God to be not only big, powerful, but good. But I came back to my darkness, crushed and without any forces stayed in bed, not moving. I remembered all our paintings, filling the house. I could not leave them, abandon them. I had to live!

CHAPTER 67

COMING BACK TO LIFE

One morning, I was in bed, not sleeping but with closed eyes. Slowly, I opened my eyelids made of lead, devastated, helpless. I glanced at the window, and I saw a tiny sunbeam. The thought crossed my mind, "The light is better than the dark." I was afraid of black. I had to have a light for the night. I was afraid of my own shadow. This time I went outside. I haven't done that in a long time.

The day was sunny, the sky was blue, deep blue. That's what my husband liked. The world was beautiful. I looked around. It was so in order and with precision, like all elements were painted by one master, one sculptor, the same engineer - it has to be some kind of God behind all this, like one great kind of computer. I was amazed. I came back home to watch TV. In the news, somebody said if you don't sleep enough, you may damage your brain. I need to live to save our legacy - somehow. I decided to have a glass of wine for the night.

Suddenly, I heard my stomach growling, and I knew I needed to start to eat, to be healthy, to do a book about us. The world should learn about the situation of artists like us - today.

I'm not driving. I asked somebody to go to the grocery store. I bought a few things, the strawberries, big and appetizing. When I chose one, I was not able to swallow any of them because I gave the best and biggest to my husband. The memory was too painful. Nothing had any taste. It had to be strong like salt or tomato sauce. Slowly, the taste was coming back. I started to take sleep pills, none of them were helping. I was changing them all the time.

I started to do a memory book. That made me even closer to him. He was the only one on this earth, so close, a family. And I had dreams. He was coming back to me and that was the consolation. Even to see his shadow for a few seconds was helping me. In dreams, he was younger and no color, always in grays.

I needed faith in my survival. Once he came in my dream, and he was passing through me like I was a spirit, with such enormous love that I never felt like this before. Another time, I saw him happy. I never saw him so happy in real life. It was because he saw God.

He was looking at something so beautiful that I was

not able to express his admiration. I didn't see God, but I had strong feelings, and that was enough to wake up and feel good. It was very assuring.

He died in the middle of the project. His life was an unfinished symphony.

THE YEAR IS 2022

My fairy tale life with him up to reality now. I am very isolated, miss him terribly. I remember the best of him. My love for him intensified. I had a good life with him. I was loved. Every life starts with love, needs love to exist and day with love.

I smile at the blue sky when thinking about him, grateful for every smile of our 50 years together. I miss him terribly. Every morning, I look at his self portrait and say Hello - time doesn't heal. I see him like yesterday. My window to the world is closed because I don't use a computer. I don't have any family. (They were all killed during World War II. Because of art, we didn't have any children - that was our sacrifice.) I don't drive. My husband said that I don't need it. It was flattering that he wanted to keep me for himself. But there's always a few good people driving me to the grocery store. They are all so busy that I don't want to bother anybody.

I keep looking to the sky. Just thinking about him makes me feel better. How good and beautiful he was. Every day, I wait for the night if I'm gonna see him in my dreams. Maybe just for a second. I am walking through my yard and feel spirit in this world pulsation, it makes me not that lonely. I need God's existence to survive. But I can't lie to myself. My reason tells me that this world has a sense, if God exists, everything is in a different perspective. I keep looking for the trace of God in this world - but world existence is a trace of him by itself, isn't it?

Existence is so good that it is almost too good to be true - but it is. Just touch with your eyes what's around - grass, snow, animals, humans - enjoy.

My priority now is to save our legacy. Our art is too important to be lost. I called big collectors. We had special talents and dreams to become great artists. We kept our promise to ourselves. But the collectors said, "you are not well-known." One said, "I prefer to go to the big museum, pay several million dollars and get a big name."

Mr. Tomilson Hill was nice to answer my letter in which he praised us. "I agree with Agnes Gund (great collector) and Arabella Makari (curator) that your work has great vitality and authenticity. Your use of color is especially vibrant and creates a very intense dynamic.

Regrettably, the paintings that you and Zbigniew Fitz have created do not fit into our collection."

That opinion gave me an idea: if we are so good, why would somebody invest in promotion? I have a very good 'product' and somebody can make a great profit from our 80 paintings. I'm not gonna ask for any money. The greater the investment, the greater the profit is going to be. Another good opinion came from an art historian (Mr. P.H.F.) who said in a letter to me: "Artwork made by you and Zbigniew Fitz require significant financial investment for development, promotion and marketing."

Now, I am almost 80 years old. Fitz's and my 80 paintings come from different stages of creativity. We departed from narrative, toward psychological expressionism. Distortions of the human body are giving a more personal approach. Display chronologically will show the progress of the mind through art.

I want to place them in the good hands of an investor, to keep them for future generations, where we don't need to fit. Our art is proof that hands are not dead, art can be done by hands.

I believe in the future, a young general is gonna feel by instinct that, "what's good, is good." We were ordinary people, but art made us extraordinary. And deep love elevated us above all.

Somebody can invest in promotion for your own profit. We have the art at:

Saatchi Gallery online under separate name: Emilia Fitz and/or Zbigniew Fitz

ABOUT THE AUTHOR

Emilia Fitz - Biography

I was born in Ukraine, raised in Poland.

During the first year at the Academy of Fine Art in Cracow, Poland, when I was 20 years old, I met Zbigniew Fitz. It was love at first sight. We became living proof of fairy tales being real. Love for art united us, our love deepening with time. We felt as a symbol what lifetime friendship can do for art. Our collaboration led to the achievement of great quality of paintings. We left Communist Poland for political reasons and took asylum in Paris.

We came to the USA in 1974 (via Paris and Montreal, Canada.) We were sponsored by one of the major textile companies from New York City, as textile designers. In 1986, we came back to France to study in European museums. Between 1987 and 1994, we had several exhibitions at the museums of the south of France, Foundation Paul Richard, Gallery in Monaco and Gallery La Spirale in Prato, Italy. In 1996, we came to the USA - it felt like coming back home, to live in Phoenix, Arizona. We had exhibitions in Los Angeles & Santa Barbara,

California and had a solo exhibition at Dinnerware Contemporary Art Gallery in Tucson, Arizona.

2001 was the turning point in our art. As we departed from narrative to the psychological inspirations toward abstraction of feelings, leading to discovery of our new form, it was psychological expressionism.

In 2006, we moved to South Carolina.

In April 2007, we had a retrospective exhibition at the Greenwood Museum in South Carolina. In the Greenwood studio, we worked full time, discovering exciting aspects of our new form.

From Greenwood, we moved twice. Each new place was a hope for a new, better life. But years of struggles damaged the body of my beautiful husband, and in 2014, he died from a heart attack - his life cut short in the middle of new projects, like unfinished symphony.

When he died, part of me died too. But I had to live to save our legacy, to place our works in good hands.

Does heaven exist or should I invent one... for my survival?

To see our art online, click our name on Google, under separate name: Saatchi Gallery online, Emilia Fitz or Zbigniew Fitz

9 781637 773833